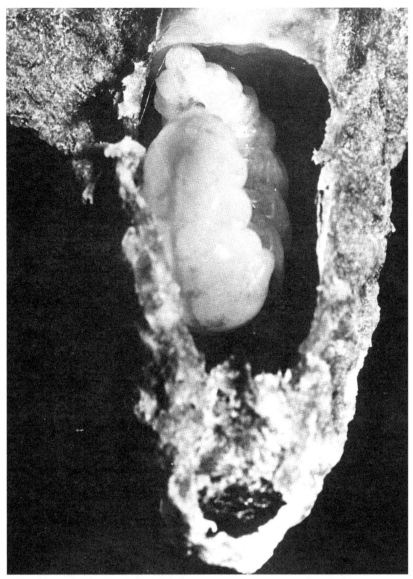

Frontispiece. Well developed and well fed larva completing feeding following spinning of the cocoon and before becoming quiet as a prepupa.

Contemporary
QUEEN REARING

By
HARRY H. LAIDLAW, JR.

FIRST EDITION

DADANT & SONS • HAMILTON, ILLINOIS

Library of Congress Catalog Card Number 79-50568
ISBN Number 0-915698-06-4

PRINTED IN THE U.S.A.

BY

ROYAL PRINTING, QUINCY, IL

Foreword

Queen rearing to many beekeepers is esoteric. To them it may seem better to leave the production of queens to those who specialize in this activity. But this is not necessarily so; a beekeeper with one colony can readily rear a replacement queen, and a beekeeper with hundreds or even thousands of colonies can rear the queens he needs without undue difficulty. Rearing a large number of queens in a short period of time for sale, however, is another matter. This requires precise scheduling and good management, specialized equipment, considerable labor, and adequate finances. Nevertheless, the principles are the same whether few queens or thousands are reared.

The purpose of this book is to instruct the beekeeper in rearing the best possible queens: as a hobby or on a commercial scale. A chapter devoted to package bee production is included because package bee production and queen rearing are so often pursued together.

I would be remiss not to recognize the founder of modern queen rearing, G. M. Doolittle, and to credit the men and women who contributed so much to our knowledge and present methods; among whom were the pioneers of the latter part of the past century and the first half of this century, and the many California and Southern States queen breeders I have worked with and visited for many years. In addition, our past and present-day scientists have contributed greatly to our understanding of queen, drone, and worker morphology and development, physiology, nutrition, behavior, and heredity. Their researches often explain the success or non-success of applied procedures, and guide us in devising better ones.

I wish to express my appreciation to Mr. Howard Veatch for supervising the publication of this book, to my wife, Ruth, for doing all the necessary typing and for critically reading the manuscript, and to my daughter, Barbara, for making Fig. 12. I am grateful, also, to my peers and former students for their suggestions, which have provoked consideration of overlooked items and reconsideration of others.

HARRY H. LAIDLAW, JR.

Davis, California
October 26, 1978

Inside Front Cover — H. C. Short, Fitzpatrick, Alabama
Front Flyleaf — J. F. McVay, Jackson, Alabama
Back Flyleaf — W. E. Harrell, Hayneville, Alabama
Inside Back Cover — C. W. Baker, Sumterville, Alabama

CONTENTS

I. THE QUEEN 1
   Role in the Colony 1
   Reproductive Tract 2
   Oviposition 4
   Origin of the Queen 7
   Mating 11
   Classification 13

II. BIOLOGICAL BASES OF REARING FULLY
    DETERMINED AND FULLY DEVELOPED
    VIRGIN QUEENS 15
    Queen Caste Determination 15
    Feeding of Larvae 18
    Conditions Favorable for Cell Building 20
    Grafting Size of Larvae 20
    Growth of Queen Cells and Larvae 21
    Prepupae 24
    Pupa 24

III. PRODUCING VIRGIN QUEENS 29
     Expedient and Hobby Queen Rearing 29
        Natural or Spontaneous Queen Cells 29
        Natural Cells With Beekeeper Control 30
     Rearing Many Queens 35
        Preparation for Rearing Virgins by the Grafting Method .. 35
        Cell Cups 35
        Obtaining Larvae 43
           The "Hunt" System 43
           Comb in Breeder Colony and to Feeder Colony 44
           Confinement of Breeder Queen to One or a
              Few Combs 45
           Breeder Queen Confined to Half-comb Insert 47
           Breeder Queen Confined to Compartment in
              Shallow or 6⅝" Depth Body 48
        Grafting 49
           Grafting Place, Humidity, Temperature, Light 49
           Grafting Into Natural Cups 51
           Grafting Into Artificial Cups 51
           Double Grafting 54
        Building the Cells 54

Starting the Cells 55
   Confined Starting Colonies 55
      Swarm Box 56
      Modified Swarm Box 59
      A Successful Variation of the
         Modified Swarm Box 61
   Free-flying Starter Colonies 61
      One-story Queenless 63
      Two-story Queenless 64
      Modification of Free-flying Starter Colony .. 64
   Finishing the Cells 66
      Queenright Finishing Colony 66
      Variation of Queenright Finisher 67
   Starter-finisher Cell Builders 68
      Queenright Starter-finisher 68
      Modification of the Usual Queenright
         Starter-finisher Colony 68
      Queenless Starter-finisher Colonies 70
  Incubator Colony 72
  Incubators 73
  Removing Bars of Cells from Frames 73
Virgin Nurseries 73
Feeders 75
Records 76

IV. MATING THE QUEEN 79
Providing Mates 79
Mating Queens from Full Size Hives 80
  Requeening 80
  Increase or "Divides" 81
Mating Colonies or Nuclei 82
  Board Divides 82
  Single Full-depth or Shallow Standard-frame Nuclei 83
  Divided Standard Hive Body Nuclei 84
  Baby Nuclei 89
Mating Yard Layout and Records 93
Severe Robbing 95
Mating Queens by Instrumental Insemination 96
  Planning the Inseminations 98
  Securing Mature Drones from Selected Drone Mothers ... 100
  Pre-insemination Care of Virgin Queens 103

Post-insemination Care of Instrumentally Inseminated
Queens 104
Introduction of Instrumentally Inseminated Queens 106
Insemination of Potential Breeding Queens for
Other Beekeepers 107

V. USE OF QUEENS 109
Caging Queens 109
Queens Caged for Package Bees 112
Queens Caged for Individual Shipment 113
Queen Cage Candy 113
Clipping and Marking 115
Recelling 116
Shipping 117
Introduction of Queens 118
Push-in Cages 118
The Miller Introducing Cage 119
Other Methods 120
Hive Records 120

VI. PACKAGE BEE PRODUCTION 121
Colony Management 121
Package Bee Supplies 123
Filling the Packages 124
Elimination of Bees Adhering to the Outside of the Cages 135
Feeding Before Shipment 136
Installation 136

VII. STOCK MAINTENANCE AND IMPROVEMENT
BY BEEKEEPERS 139
Maintenance of the Characteristics of a Stock 140
Improvement of Stock by the Beekeeper 141
Colony Descriptions or Profiles 141
Individual Queen Record 142
Yard Sheet 146
Biological Phenomena Underlying Bee Breeding 148
Origin and Maturation of Eggs 148
Origin and Maturation of Spermatozoa 149
Functioning or Expression of Genes 150
Relationships of Individuals Within a Colony 151
The Queen 151
The Workers 152

The Drones 152
Queen Mated to One Drone 152
Queen Mated to Several Drones from Different
    Mothers 153
Queen Mated to Several Drones from the Same
    Mother 153
Queen Mated to Drones from Several Mothers and
    Also to Some Drones Having the Same Mother .. 154
Significance of Honey Bee Relationships 154
Beekeeper Management of Test Colonies 155

VIII. A BRIEF HISTORY OF QUEEN REARING 159
Bee Biology that is Basic to Queen Rearing 159
    Queen and Worker Castes 159
    Drones and Parthenogenesis 161
    Drones and Fertilization of the Egg 161
    Mating of the Queen 162
    Recognition by the Queen of Worker and Drone Cells 164
Emergence of Queen Rearing as a Beekeeping Practice 165
Development of Queen Rearing as a Commercial
    Beekeeping Activity 166
    Rearing Virgin Queens 166
        Obtaining and Preparing Larvae for Cell Builders 167
        Building the Cells 168
    Mating the Queens 171
    Shipping Queens 175
In Retrospect 177

REFERENCES 177

INDEX 187

Contemporary
QUEEN REARING

CHAPTER I

The Queen

Role in the Colony

There is only one queen in a honey bee colony which may consist of up to 60,000 workers and up to several thousand drones, yet both bees and beekeepers attach the greatest importance to her presence; there is good reason for this:

First, she is the mother of all other individuals in the colony. She may live several years, but worker bees live only a few weeks during the active season and without their constant replacement the colony dies.

Second, she is the custodian of the male parents' contributions to the heredity of her female offspring, as well as contributing her own, and thus she is responsible for the characteristics of the colony.

Third, her presence is intimately associated with the "morale" of the colony and is known to the bees by their sharing of her pheromones. Pheromones are chemical substances produced in the body but released outside the body to incite particular reactions in others of the same species. The absence of the queen causes obvious distress among the workers of a colony, and a colony without a queen, said to be "queenless," exhibits behavior different from a colony with a queen, a "queenright" colony (Laidlaw 1975).

Though the queen is the mother of the colony and a very efficient producer of eggs she is devoid of maternal instinct and is physically unable to care for her young. She lacks the glands that secrete the larval food and the glands that secrete wax for cell building. Her legs are not fitted for pollen collection and transport. She thus must share the duties of motherhood with the workers which are capable of nursing and other colony duties. It is this sharing that permits the specialization necessary for the growth of large populations of worker bees essential for the life and prosperity of the colony.

The queen (Fig. 1), with her large thorax and large abdomen that is shaped and colored differently from that of workers and drones, stands out in the colony as a special bee. It is only natural that her existence as the only one of her kind in a colony and the attention bestowed upon her by attendant worker bees would lead early beekeepers to consider her a ruler of the colony. Rulers of human societies were most often kings, and, although Aristotle mentioned that some beekeepers of his time called her the mother of the colony (Artistotle), she was thought of as a king

[*1*]

Fig. 1. An easily recognizable mother queen among her workers and drones on a brood comb.

until Charles Butler in 1609 identified her sex as female. Her role in the colony was still believed to be that of a ruler and only her title was changed with this discovery. We know today that the queen's presence influences the behavior of worker bees but she does not direct the activities of the colony. The name for this female caste, though inaccurate, is secure in beekeeping terminology and appropriately sets apart a remarkable bee.

Reproductive Tract

The reproductive tract of the queen (Snodgrass 1956; Fig. 2) is fully developed and very efficient, in contrast to the vestigial nature of the reproductive tract of the worker. It consists of a pair of large ovaries located in the sides of the anterior part of the abdomen and a pair of expandable lateral oviducts leading from the ovaries to a single median oviduct that terminates in an anterio-posteriorly flattened pouch, the vagina. The vagina opens beneath the sting into the bursa copulatrix within the sting chamber.

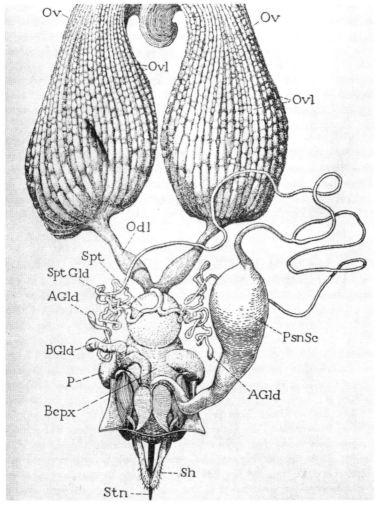

Fig. 2. Reproductive system and sting of the queen honey bee, dorsal view. AGld, acid gland of sting; Bcpx, bursa copulatrix; BGld, accessary gland of sting; Odl, lateral oviduct; Ov, ovary; Ovl, ovarioles; P, lateral pouch of bursa copulatrix; PsnSc, poison sac of sting; Sh, sheath lobes of sting; Spt, spermatheca; SptGld, spermathecal glands; Stn, shaft of sting. (From Snodgrass 1956).

A spherical sperm reservoir or spermatheca, about 1 mm in diameter, lies dorsal to the vagina and is connected to the anterio-dorsal wall of the vagina by a slender spermathecal duct having a muscular "S"-shaped valve that governs passage of sperm into and out of the spermatheca. Two glands applied to the sides of the spermatheca open into the spermathecal duct near its junction with the spermatheca and are intimately involved in its function. The spermatheca is encased in a tracheal envelope that apparently functions to protect the sperm from extreme variations in temperature (Flanders 1977).

A transverse invagination arises from the ventral side of the vagina at its junction with the median oviduct and is situated beneath the opening of the spermathecal duct. This is the valvefold. Outside of the reproductive tract proper and enclosed in the sting chamber is the sting, the basal part of which is instrumental in transporting the egg from the vagina to the cell bottom during oviposition (Briant 1927; Laidlaw, unpublished).

Oviposition

The eggs are formed in the ovaries each of which is composed of a bundle of parallel slender membranous tubules or ovarioles that converge sharply at their posterior ends; some to unite before opening into the expanded anterior ends of the paired lateral oviducts. Eckert (1934) found in one study that the number of ovarioles in both ovaries varied among queens from 260 to 373. Assuming an average of 325 ovarioles for both ovaries, a queen laying 1200 eggs a day would produce 3.7 eggs per ovariole each 24 hours, though two days or more may be required for the formation of the egg. If the queen laid at the rate of 1500 eggs per day, the eggs would be produced at the rate of 4.6 eggs per ovariole.

The eggs originate from primary germ cells in the slender anterior tip of each ovariole. They progress toward the ovariole base and a group of nurse cells forms and follows them in the ovariole (Snodgrass 1956; Fig. 3). Both the growing egg and the nurse cells become enclosed in a cellular envelope, but the egg and nurse cells are in chambers separated by a sphincter-like constriction of the cellular envelope between the two chambers through the center of which a bit of the egg abuts against the nurse cells. As the egg nears the basal end of the ovariole it suddenly consumes the nurse cells and reaches full size. The cellular envelope now secretes the egg shell or chorion leaving the imprints of the cells on the egg surface and a micropylar opening in the place where the egg protoplasm projected into the nurse cell chamber. This opening is where the sperm will enter the egg to fertilize it. The envelope, or the egg itself, secretes also a sticky substance on the posterior end of the egg which will

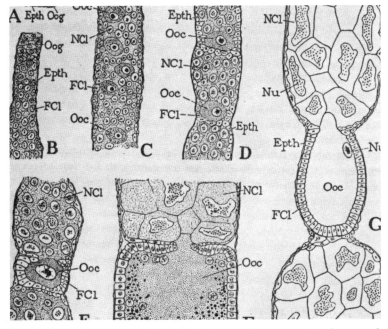

Fig. 3. Oogenesis or egg origin and development in an ovariole of a queen's ovary. Epth, epithelium; Fcl, follicle cell; NCL, nurse cell; Nu, nucleus; Ooc, oocyte; Oog, oogonium. (From Snodgrass 1956).

adhere the egg to the cell bottom. Several eggs may be held briefly in the expandable lateral oviducts.

Research has not yet definitely established exactly how the egg receives sperm as it is laid, but the morphology of the reproductive tract and observations by biologists (Adam 1913) suggests that as the egg passes through the vagina the valvefold presses the micropyle against the opening of the spermathecal duct so one or more sperm may enter if the egg is to become a female. One sperm will unite with the egg nucleus to form a zygote. If the egg is not to be fertilized, the valvefold is retracted allowing the egg to bypass the duct. The egg nucleus in this case soon undergoes division without union with a sperm.

That the queen can control the sex of her offspring is amazing to those little acquainted with honey bees. She does this simply by fertilizing an egg with a spermatozoon from her spermatheca as the egg is laid if the egg is to develop into a female, and laying the egg without fertilization if it is to develop into a male.

Dzierzon in 1845 stated from experimental evidence that drones develop from unfertilized eggs. Recently it has been shown that drones can also originate from fertilized eggs under certain circumstances and are thus diploid as are the females, but these drones do not survive beyond a few hours as larvae in colonies because they are eaten by the workers, and this causes "spotty" brood because of the empty cells among cells with brood (Woyke 1963a, 1963b). Not all spotty brood is due to bees eating diploid drone larvae; other causes of spotty brood are cannibalism (Garófalo 1977; Woyke 1977) and the queen's missing some cells during oviposition.

The queen is guided in whether to lay a fertilized or unfertilized egg by the size of the comb cell which she measures with her forelegs as she inspects the cell (Koeniger 1970). Fertilized eggs are also laid in natural queen cell cups which are larger than worker cells, but these cells open downward and their position may influence the queen. In addition, environmental and seasonal changes influence whether eggs are laid in worker, drone, or queen cells, and whether they and the larvae that hatch from them are cared for or are removed by the worker bees. In fact, whether eggs are laid at all depends on the queen's receiving from the workers the kind of food that is necessary for egg development. The workers in this way control oviposition and correlate it with seasonal and environmental conditions.

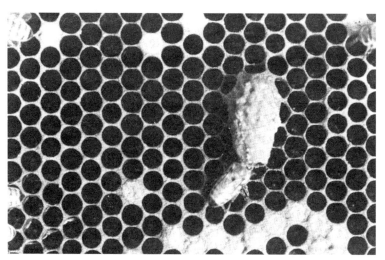

Fig. 4. A developing and unsealed natural queen cell. It is extended downward by the workers as the larva grows.

The queen may lay as many as 1500 eggs in a 24-hour period, and perhaps somewhat more, though often queens will lay less at their peak of egg production. This is a rate of more than one egg each minute. The queen lays several eggs rapidly and then rests and feeds from the mouths of attendant workers that surround her and supply her with royal jelly and honey. The queen can feed herself from honey in the comb or from queen cage candy and will do so when she is caged, but she can get the royal jelly only from worker bees that are secreting it.

Origin of the Queen

Queens are reared in nature in special cells that extend downward from the face or edges of the comb (Fig. 4). The cells originate in two ways: from small natural cell cups (Fig. 5) that are usually present in hives, or, when a colony has lost its queen, by the enlargement of worker cells that contain young, and as yet undifferentiated, larvae. The queen lays in the natural cups when the colony is preparing to swarm or when the old queen will be superseded by a young queen. These queens are reared from the egg as are all naturally reared queens except those reared by a colony that has lost its queen by disease or accident. Accidental loss

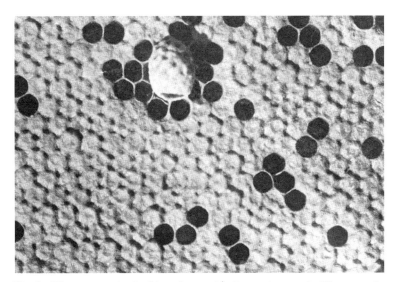

Fig. 5. The presence in the hive of natural cell cups is normal. These may be the bases of former queen cells, or they may have been constructed anew by the workers.

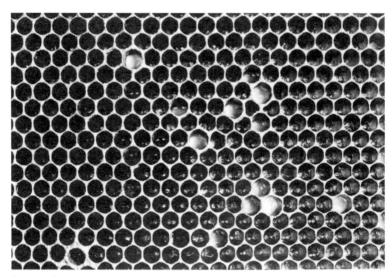

Fig. 6. Queenless colonies will select certain very young larvae in worker cells to become queens. The larvae are supplied with abundant quantities of royal jelly and the cell walls are flared.

of queens is unlikely in feral colonies. When a colony loses its queen, some of the young worker larvae receive such a quantity of royal jelly they are floated to the opening of the worker cell. The cell walls are flared (Fig. 6) and the queen cell is turned downward as the bees continue its development (Fig. 7).

The virgin emerges about 16 days after the egg was laid. She soon seeks out cells with queens nearly ready to emerge and begins their destruction by cutting a hole in the side. She may sting the inmate through the hole she made. The bees complete the destruction of the cell, and such cells always have a ragged opening in the side (Figs. 8, 9). Cells from which virgins emerged have a round hole in the end where the virgin cut off the capping (Fig. 10). Virgins pay little attention to unsealed queen cells and these are soon destroyed by the workers.

Should other virgins emerge they fight when they meet (Fig. 11) until finally only one survives. This is likely to occur if inclement weather has made the bees postpone swarming. The bees may hold the virgins in their cells until the swarm emerges, feeding them through the opening between the cap and the cell. Both virgins that are held in queen cells and those that have emerged may emit "piping" sounds that are thought to be challenges to other virgins.

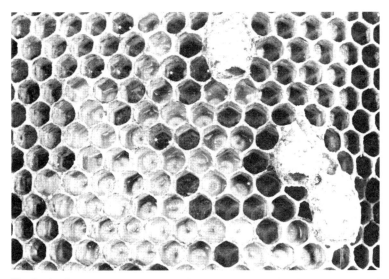

Fig. 7. As the larva grows in a natural queen cell originating from a worker cell, the cell is turned downward over the comb surface.

Fig. 8. A natural queen cell that has been destroyed by the bees following emergence of a virgin queen from another queen cell.

Fig. 9. Sealed grafted queen cells that have been destroyed because of the presence of an unconfined queen in the hive. Such cells have the cap at the end of the cell intact, and there is a hole in the side through which the bees removed the inmate.

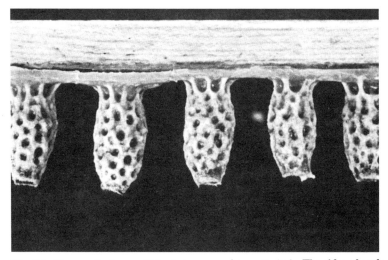

Fig. 10. Queen cells from which virgin queens have emerged. The sides of each cell are intact and the cap at the end has been cut off by the emerging queen.

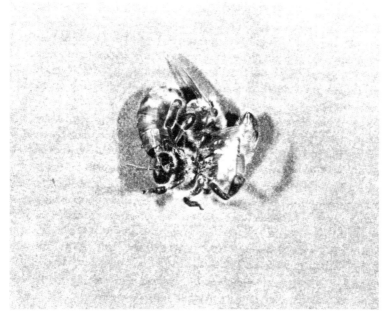

Fig. 11. Virgins will fight when they meet in the colony.

Mating

The virgin takes a mating flight when about seven days old, though she may make a brief flight before her mating flight. She will mate with several drones, possibly an average of 7 to 10 or more and a maximum of about 20. If she mated with few drones on this flight she may make another mating flight the same day, or she may make one or more subsequent mating flights the next day, or even later. She begins laying three or four days following mating. Thus, commercial queen breeders expect to harvest laying queens from nuclei 14 or 15 days after the nuclei received queen cells.

All of the sperm produced by a drone are formed before his emergence. When the drone emerges from the cell, the tubules of the very large testes are filled with sperm, but the drone cannot mate until the sperm move into the seminal vesicles which are a pair of heavily muscled and tracheated epithelial tubes situated between the testes and the ejaculatory duct (Snodgrass 1956). If the young drone is properly fed and remains in the broodnest where the temperature is favorable (Jaycox 1961), the sperm move into the seminal vesicles where they attach themselves to the epithelial wall and remain until they are ejaculated at mating (Bishop 1920). As the sperm migrate to the seminal vesicles the testes degenerate until finally they are no more than mere bits of amorphous tissue. The process of sperm migration, or drone maturing, requires 8 to 10 days. When drones are mature they tend to move from the active broodnest to the side combs.

The drone dies at mating. The eversion of the copulatory organ brought about by violent contraction of the abdominal muscles and followed by the contraction of the muscles of the seminal vesicles and then those of the mucus glands ruptures the reproductive tract.

Tryasko (1975) and Woyke and Ruttner (1958) presented an excellent account of how the drone and queen copulate and explained the origin of the "mating sign" and the manner in which the queen separates from the drone. There still remained the question as to how subsequent drones mated with a queen whose sting chamber was filled with mucus and the remnants of the endophallus of a drone that mated before.

Laidlaw (1944, and unpublished), from a study of the mechanics of mating, formulated the hypothesis that as the copulatory organ of the drone everts explosively into the open sting chamber of the queen the everting cornua penetrate the lateral space between the anterior membrane of the sting chamber and the body wall and are held in place momentarily by their expansion and by an orange colored sticky substance that covers the distal surface of the everted cornua. As it everts, the endophallus, which is the central part of the copulatory organ and when fully everted bears at its tip the orifice of the ejaculatory duct or gonopore, pushes along the underside of the sting shaft of the queen and into and through a channel formed by the bases of the two oblong plates of the sting which is lined by a membrane having short, setal protuberances. This membranous lining is the remnant of the sternum of body segment IX (Snodgrass 1956) that became modified as the morphology of the bee changed over the years. As eversion continues, the tip of the endophallus reaches the bursa copulatrix and curls ventrally entering the vagina and pushing the valvefold from over the median oviduct orifice. The endophallus enlarges and by its enlargement is pushed out of the vagina as the lumen of the bulb opens by the pulling away of the penis membrane that covers the tips of the sclerotized plates, but is held firmly against the vaginal orifice by the cornua; and violent ejaculation of semen takes place followed by the ejaculation of mucus. Eversion continues, and following ejaculation, the penis bulb slips out of the incompletely everted penis (Woyke and Ruttner 1958) and remains in the sting chamber as the "mating sign." The eversion of the endophallus continues without pause and the cornua are pulled out before the penis reaches full eversion, sometimes leaving remnants of the sticky orange covering on the mating sign. The immobilized and dying drone drops away with the fully everted endophallus intact but the sclerotized plates are missing.

After it was conclusively shown that the queen mates with several drones on one mating flight the perplexing question arose as to how drones that mate with the queen following the first one manage to do so since the sting chamber is filled with the mating sign. Laidlaw (unpublished) hypothesized that the second and subsequent drones mate with the queen as did the first. The queen mates with drones in rapid succession. The mucus of the mating sign is still fluid as subsequent drones mount the flying queen, and as the penis of the copulating drone expands and lengthens on full eversion, it dislodges the mating sign of the preceding drone and the drone leaves his own. The queen returns to the hive bearing the mating sign of the last drone with which she mated.

Classification

Queen breeders have for many years classified the queens they sell (Murry 1921) as *untested, tested, select tested* and *breeders.* The *untested* classification is the usual one for almost all queens sold; the terms *tested* and *select tested* are now rarely used.

Untested queens are simply queens that are laying in queen mating nuclei. If queens have been instrumentally inseminated, they may have been permitted to lay or may have been held for some time in cages in nursery colonies before shipment.

Tested queens have been held in nuclei until their emerging bees can be observed to determine whether they have "mismated" with drones of another race. When the black bee, *Apis mellifera mellifera,* was common in the United States, breeders of Italian bees, *Apis mellifera ligustica,* experienced considerable difficulty in preventing their Italian queens from mating with at least some black drones. The customers were not pleased with this situation, believing, as did nearly everyone, that a queen mates with one drone, and, therefore, if there were evidence of mismating all of the queen's workers would be race hybrids and it would be impossible to continue the Italian race by breeding from her. The queen breeders met this objection by offering higher priced tested queens.

Select tested queens are supposedly tested in colonies for a season for various characteristics, including honey production.

Breeding queens are those that have been used by the queen rearer as breeders, and their daughters have been tested in producing colonies for a season or more and found to be excellent. Breeding queens are costly and because of age are subject to supersedure soon after the buyer receives them.

A beekeeper can select breeding queens from within his own stock and from among untested queens bought from several queen breeders for comparative observation in his own yards. Both queen mothers and drone mothers should be selected. Initially, the queen mothers and drone mothers should preferably not come from the same stock.

The best queens can be reared only from good stock. But even the best stock will not produce good queens if the queen rearing methods that are used fail to provide the developing queen with adequate and proper food, and with other environmental necessities, from at least the time the egg hatches.

CHAPTER II

Biological Bases of Rearing Fully Determined and Fully Developed Virgin Queens

Queen Caste Determination

Our first consideration in rearing queen bees is: how do queens become queens? We should be aware of at least the outlines of how queens originate and the factors in the environment that impinge upon the formation of a queen bee, especially those that exert considerable influence on the development of queen characteristics, so we may be guided in devising beekeeping methods that will consistently produce excellent queens. As we know, any fertilized egg can normally give rise to either a queen or a worker, and each of these female castes has physical, physiological, and behavioral characteristics not shared by the other. The larva that hatches from a fertilized egg can progress toward becoming a queen or a worker (Fig. 12), and though there is, of course, an underlying genetic basis, it is well established that the course it takes depends upon the food it receives. This fact is central to queen rearing. It should be noted that neither the queen nor the worker can be considered the "perfect" caste and the other a deviant and underdeveloped modification. Both, in the evolution of the honey bee colony and its individuals, have developed from the ancient ancestral form which supposedly could perform all of the functions now shared by queen and worker.

When the egg is laid it is a single, large, elongate cell, visually uncomplicated (Fig. 13). For about the next 72 to 74 hours at brood nest temperature great activity takes place within the egg. The fertilized nucleus divides shortly after the egg is laid to initiate subsequent nuclear divisions and formation of new minute cells, each enclosed in a cell membrane within the egg shell, that form the tissues and organs of the larva (Nelson 1915). This activity is embryogeny, or embryogenesis, and when the larva is fully formed it secretes a liquid to partially dissolve the egg shell and then wriggles free (DuPraw 1961). It now begins its postembryonic development and must have food, which previously was the yolk of the egg, supplied by nurse bees.

The larva upon hatching is neither a queen larva nor a worker larva. It is uncommitted at this point to become either caste though normally

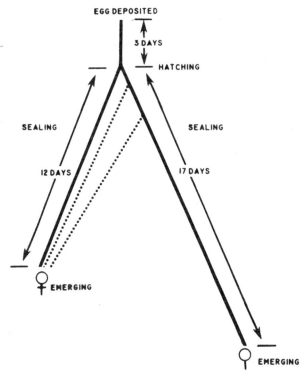

EGG DEPOSITED

3 DAYS

HATCHING

SEALING

SEALING

12 DAYS

17 DAYS

♀ EMERGING

♀ EMERGING

Fig. 12. Divergence of developmental paths of queen and worker larvae.

The larva that hatches from a fertilized egg may become either a queen or a worker. If it is in a worker cell it begins to develop into a worker as soon as it begins to eat. However, it remains capable of becoming an acceptable queen for the first one and one-half days of its larval life, and if transferred to a queen cell cup during that period and placed in an environment where it will receive an adequate amount of proper food it will develop into a queen that is difficult, if not impossible, to distinguish from queens reared entirely in queen cells. This capability is indicated by the top dotted line in the diagram.

When a larva has progressed toward becoming a worker for a somewhat longer period, its direction of development can still be changed but the resulting adult will be to some degree an intercaste, whether visually recognizable or not, as is illustrated by the lower dotted line of the diagram.

Both queen and worker larvae feed for only six days. Since food is the principal factor in female caste determination and development, it is readily apparent that if the initial half of a larva's feeding activity is directed toward the larva's becoming a worker, the larva will have advanced so far in that direction it can become only an intercaste when a changed environment alters the developmental direction toward that of becoming a queen.

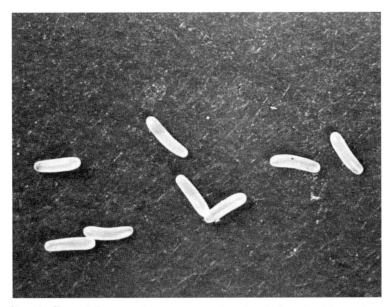

Fig. 13. Eggs of the queen bee are sausage-shaped and about 1 millimeter long. The egg shell or chorion is flexible and bears the imprints of the follicle cells that secreted it.

it has the potential, in the proper environment, to develop into a fully developed queen or a fully developed worker. As soon as it begins to eat it starts its progress toward becoming one caste or the other. The food of queen and worker larvae differs somewhat, and the sugar content governs the rate of food intake which is higher in queen larvae than in worker larvae. Rate of food intake regulates the activity of the corpora allata, and thereby the amount of juvenile hormone produced. The level of JH regulates the processes leading to the development of the two castes; a high level during the third day of larval development induces differentiation into a queen (Beetsma 1979).

A genetically influenced threshold of larval response to food composition was suggested by Weaver (1966), and is given credence by the rare occurrence of intercastes from some queen cells with highly inbred larvae (Laidlaw, unpublished).

It is of theoretical and practical importance to know how far a larva can progress toward becoming a worker before it reaches a point in caste development that precludes altering this direction toward becoming an acceptable queen, though this queen may be to some degree an intercaste.

It has been shown that queens reared from larvae that began their development toward queens upon hatching had more ovarioles in the ovaries than those that were developing for even a few hours toward becoming workers (Woyke 1971). This research indicates that the most perfect queens must be reared from very young larvae, but whether the additional ovarioles would contribute to significantly better practical performance than that of queens reared from 12 to 24 hour old larvae is unknown and the extra cost in producing such queens is an important economic consideration.

It seems clear that the beginning of determination of the queen caste takes place early in larval development, but it is not yet known whether inadequate feeding in the latter part of larval growth and development influences continuing caste differentiation and results in an intercaste or in merely a fully caste determined but small queen. It has been observed, however, that cells that are started in poorly maintained cell builders and finished in excellently maintained cell builders may produce queens inferior to those produced when conditions are reversed, and that cells that were double grafted when the cells were two or three days old may produce queens that are smaller than their sisters produced from single grafted cells (Laidlaw, unpublished).

Feeding of Larvae

Since food is the critical element in the determination of the queen caste and in the development of this caste to its full potential, we must design our cell building operation so that all larvae that are to become queens are fed abundantly with proper food from the time they hatch from the egg until they finish eating in the sealed cell. This is a period of six days, but the nurses have less than five days to supply the food before the cell is sealed (Table 1) and only four days in the queen cell when larvae are grafted or otherwise prepared for cell building. This food is royal jelly, secreted by the nurse bees, and honey.

Nurse bees are normally younger bees that are not yet foragers, and they also perform additional tasks in the hive. Soon after emergence, worker bees eat stored pollen, or "bee bread," a term known even by Aristotle in the Fourth century B.C., which develops their fat bodies and causes the hypopharyngeal or brood food glands in their heads to secrete at least the main components of royal jelly. They must continue to eat pollen as long as they secrete royal jelly and feed the queen larvae. Bees do not relocate pollen in the hive as they do honey (Taber 1973; Doull 1974) so the pollen supply should be as near the cells being fed as possible, and should be supplemented by incoming pollen either as a pollen flow

TABLE 1. Length of Developmental Stages of the Honey Bee

	Workers		Queens		Drones	
Day	Stages	Moults	Stages	Moults	Stages	Moults
1						
2	Egg		Egg		Egg	
3						
4	———— 1st larval	(hatching) 1st moult	———— 1st larval	(hatching) 1st moult	———— 1st larval	(hatching) 1st moult
5	2nd larval	2nd moult	2nd larval	2nd moult	2nd larval	2nd moult
6	———— 3rd larval	3rd moult	———— 3rd larval	3rd moult	———— 3rd larval	3rd moult
7	4th larval	4th moult	4th larval	4th moult	4th larval	4th moult
8	———— Gorging	(sealing)	———— Gorging	(sealing)		
9					Gorging	
10	Pre-pupa		Pre-pupa ————	5th moult		(sealing)
11	————	5th moult				
12					Pre-pupa	
13			Pupa			
14					————	5th moult
15	Pupa					
16			———— Imago	6th moult (emerging)		
17						
18					Pupa	
19						
20	————	6th moult				
21	Imago	(emerging)				
22					————	6th moult
23					Imago	
24						(emerging)

Modified from Bertholf, L. M. 1925. The moults of the honeybee. Journal of Economic Entomology 18(2):380-384.

or as fed pollen. Cell builders should be fed 40:60 sugar syrup (40 parts of sugar: 60 parts of water by volume) continuously, or by placement of honey below the cell building area which the bees will transfer above to simulate a nectar flow.

Conditions Favorable for Cell Building

In the yearly sequence of honey bee activities swarming time in the spring is when queen cells are spontaneously built by the bees. Bees that are building such cells will build cells prepared by the beekeeper even though the colony may have its own laying queen present. Colonies that are preparing to swarm, as evidenced by building queen cells, are usually strong, often crowded, have an abundance of young bees, and there is often a light to moderate nectar and pollen flow. If any of these elements is lacking it must be provided or simulated for satisfactory cell building, whether the cell builder is preparing to swarm, is superseding its queen, or is queenless, which are the three conditions under which bees spontaneously build queen cells.

Grafting Size of Larvae

Most queens reared under the control of the beekeeper develop in beeswax artificial cell cups into which young larvae are transferred from worker cells, a process known as "grafting." One of the first questions that arises for the beginning queen rearer is how young, or small, should the larvae be that are grafted. The age as given in bee books and papers on queen rearing varies from 12 to 36 hours, with some authors preferring even younger larvae.

Some larvae may grow faster than others the same age. Whether this difference in growth rate is a manifestation of genetic or environmental differences, and whether more rapid early growth is a prognosticator of desirable adult differences should be left to the bee geneticist to determine. The queen rearer should choose larvae as young as can be transferred to queen cell cups with reasonable ease and without injury. Larvae 36 hours old should be the maximum age for grafting. The hatching of eggs may be timed so larvae are the right age, or, as is often the case, larvae may be selected that are a size considered to represent the right age. When a larva hatches, it is the size of the egg (Fig. 14). It eats larval food supplied by nurse bees and grows, stretching its cuticle or skin, until when it becomes about 1½ times the size of the egg it is a convenient size for grafting (Fig. 15). When the larva is about 16 hours old it moults or sheds its first cuticle which can be stretched

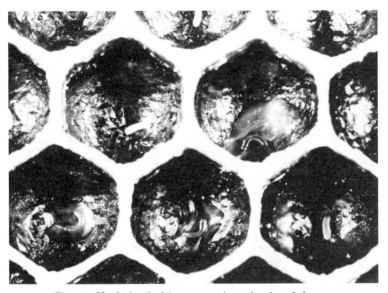

Fig. 14. Newly hatched larvae are about the size of the egg.

no more, and reveals a new cuticle that had formed beneath the old one. The larva continues to eat and grow until the second cuticle will allow no further growth, when it too is discarded. This process continues at about 24 hour intervals until the larva has moulted 4 times (Table 1). In addition to being very young, a larva chosen to become a queen should be resting on a bed of royal jelly that covers at least one-third of the area of the bottom of the worker cell (Fig. 15).

Growth of Queen Cells and Larvae

Queen cells with properly cared for larvae 24 hours following grafting have been evenly enlarged, or "drawn out," and are copiously supplied with royal jelly (Fig. 16a). Small cells, uneven growth of cells or larvae, or mis-shapen cells indicate a poorly functioning cell builder. Queens from such cells will be unsatisfactory. Cells 48 hours old are now about ⅔ the length they will attain and the basal third is filled with jelly (Fig. 16b). Four days from grafting, the cell is fully formed and is being sealed (Fig. 16d). Shortly after the cell is sealed the larva spins a cocoon in the lower half of the sealed cell (Fig. 17). When this is completed the larva finishes eating (Fig. 18) and straightens out with the head

Fig. 15. Copiously fed larvae about 20 hours old, the right size and age for grafting. The maximum size for grafting is about 1½ times the size of the egg.

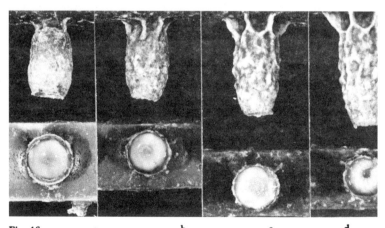

Fig. 16.   a   b   c   d

Growth of queen cells and larvae: (a) cell and larva one day from grafting; (b) two days; (c) three days; (d) four days.

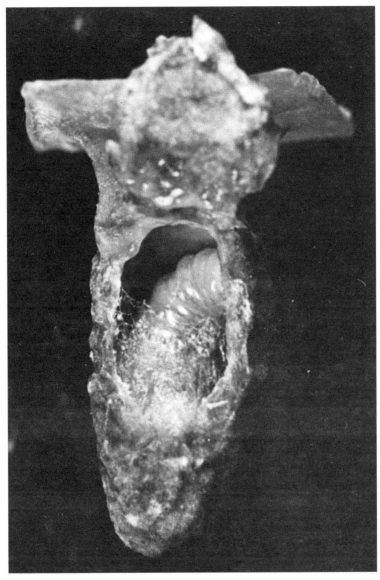

Fig. 17. The larva of a newly sealed queen cell spins a cocoon in the lower part of the cell.

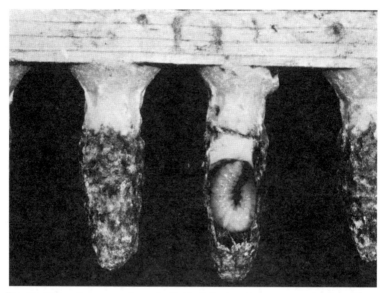

Fig. 18. When the cocoon is nearly finished the larva resumes avid feeding on the royal jelly.

directed downward and becomes quiet (Fig. 19). The larva is known now as a prepupa, though it still looks very much like a larva.

Prepupa

The prepupal period of one day (Table 1) appears to be one of quiet resting. Actually it is a time of great internal activity. Larval tissues and organs are reconstructed into pupal structures, a process that began earlier, and at about the end of the 6th day from grafting the 5th moult takes place. As the prepupal cuticle is shed the pupa is suddenly revealed with the body segments and appendages clearly in evidence.

Pupa

The pupa is at first white and very fragile (Fig. 20). For the next five days it remains visably quiet as the adult tissues and organs take form, but color changes become apparent and progress rapidly (Jay 1962; Fig. 21; Table 2). On the 5th day of the pupal form slight appendage movements begin, and the pupa moults revealing the developed queen, except the wings are still folded as pads. Soon thereafter the wings expand

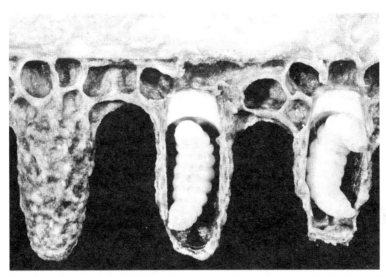

Fig. 19. After completing feeding the larva stretches out in the cell with the head downward and becomes quiet. It is now called a prepupa.

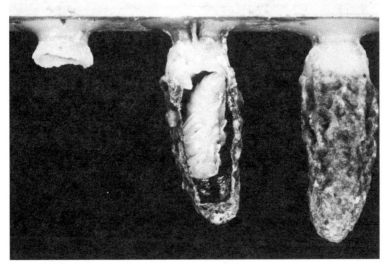

Fig. 20. The last larval skin is shed revealing the pupal form with its legs, antennae, and body divisions. It is white at this stage.

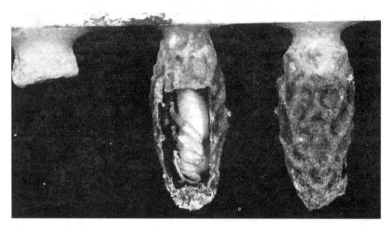

Fig. 21. Color soon appears in the eyes and body wall of the pupa and deepens progressively each day.

TABLE 2. Color Changes in Queen Pupae.

No. days from pupation	Color	Parts
1	light pink	compound eyes
2	light pink	ocelli
	medium pink	compound eyes
3	light pink-purple	compound eyes
	light yellow	head, thorax, mandibles
	dark pink	ocelli
4	light yellow	abdomen, legs, antennae
	light brown	head, thorax, leg joints, claws, stings, sutures outlining mesonotum
	dark pink-purple	compound eyes, ocelli
	dark brown	mandibles
5	light grey	wing pads
	medium grey	head, thorax
	dark yellow to light brown	abdomen, legs, frons, clypeus, tongue, scapes, pedicelli
	dark brown	leg joints, claws, sting, mandibles, spines, spurs, hair, sutures outlining mesonotum
	black	compound eyes, ocelli, flagellar segments
6		pupal moult complete

Reprinted from Table 1 of "Colour changes in honeybee pupae" by S. C. Jay, Bee World **43**(4):119-122 (1962).

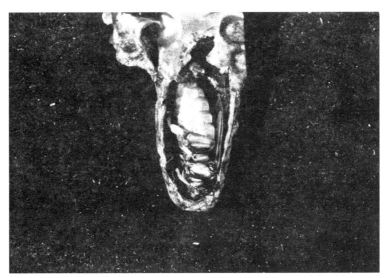

Fig. 22. Just before emergence the pupa sheds the pupal skin. The wings expand and the queen has the adult appearance.

Fig. 23. The setae or "hair" of the newly emerged queen may be somewhat damp and matted and the wings have not yet hardened.

(Fig. 22), and the adult queen emerges on the 11th or 12th day from grafting (Fig. 23). Rough handling of queen cells before the wings have expanded can bruise the wing pads and result in deformed wings. Exposure of the cells to abnormal temperatures can also damage the wing pads.

CHAPTER III

Producing Virgin Queens

For more than a century beekeepers have endeavored to induce bees to build queen cells for use when they are needed for requeening, for increase, or for sale. It is little wonder that various methods to accomplish this have been developed during this time by beekeepers who had little or no contact with each other. Some of the more articulate beekeepers published their methods in journals or books and thus influenced others, but even today experimentation continues.

Some of these methods are more suitable for a particular kind of beekeeping operation than others, but to be successful in producing excellent queens all must be based upon the proper feeding of the newly hatched larva from hatching to the end of the feeding period.

Many good methods to induce bees to build queen cells and to feed the larvae properly and adequately are currently in use. Sometimes the differences between methods are slight; in other cases the differences are major. The methods presented here are representative of those that are considered to be the better ones, and in some cases minor variations are presented if it seems likely they may be of interest. Most of the great many variations that have been published, or are in use, have been omitted as offering no improvement over the methods included.

Expedient and Hobby Queen Rearing

Perhaps the beekeeper most timid about queen rearing is the hobby beekeeper. Without some experience, rearing needed queens can seem to be beyond the beekeeper's ability. But any beekeeper, large or small, can readily rear the queens that are needed.

Natural or Spontaneous Queen Cells

From early times beekeepers have utilized queen cells built spontaneously by the bees, usually by colonies preparing to swarm, to requeen their colonies or to provide queens for additional colonies. The old queen may be removed from a colony that is building cells and one cell left to provide a young replacement queen. Surplus cells, usually sealed ones, can be cut from the comb and attached to combs in colonies from which the queens have been removed, or a comb with cells may be exchanged for one in the colony to be requeened. This is perhaps the easiest way for a hobby beekeeper to requeen his colonies. However, this method of cell building has the disadvantage of dependency on bees' building natural cells, and on the limited possibility of breeding from selected queens.

Natural Cells With Beekeeper Control

The simplest way to rear queens with greater beekeeper control is to remove the queen from a colony, or cage her away from the broodnest area; or place a comb with eggs and young larvae from a selected breeder queen into a queenless colony. The bees do the rest. Certain larvae in worker comb are selected by the bees to be fed as queen larvae. Royal jelly is placed in the cells in such abundance the larvae are floated to the mouth of the cells. At the same time, the cell walls are flared (Fig. 6). Before the larvae reach the opening of the worker cells, the queen cell walls are turned downward (Fig. 7). Good queens often emerge from these "emergency" cells; but the queens may be poor if the bees select larvae that are too old, as they sometimes do.

A small modification of this method that is more consistent in providing good queens is to select several proper size and abundantly fed larvae in worker comb and flare the cell walls around them, or remove some comb directly below the larvae selected. The bees in a colony made queenless several hours earlier will often construct queen cells where the beekeeper wants them. New comb, or comb in which only a few cycles of brood have been reared, is preferable to old dark combs for this method.

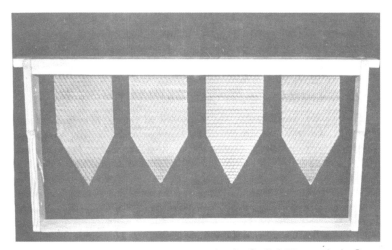

Fig. 24. Frame prepared for rearing queens by the C. C. Miller method. Queen cells will be built along the tapered margins and sometimes on the face of the comb.

Dr. C. C. Miller (1912) took advantage of the natural proclivity of queenless bees to rear queens from young larvae in worker comb by giving them a specially prepared frame of newly hatched larvae. The frame is prepared with several strips of foundation, two or three inches wide and nearly as long as the frame is deep. These are tapered to a point at one end and fastened at the other end to the top bar of an empty frame (Fig. 24). The prepared frame is then put into the broodnest of a selected breeder colony. About a week later the bees will have drawn out the foundation, and the comb will contain brood, with eggs and the youngest larvae toward the edges. The comb is now ready for preparation for the cell building colony.

Two or three hours before it is to be used, a cell building colony should be prepared from a strong colony by transferring the queen and two frames of the youngest brood with adhering bees to another hive body, leaving a space in the middle of the broodnest of the strong and now queenless colony for the comb from the breeder queen. When the bees of the cell builder have become aware of the loss of their queen, the prepared comb is removed from the breeder colony and, after a gentle shake to dislodge most of the bees, the remaining bees are brushed gently from the new comb. Care must be taken because new comb is fragile and in this case is not supported by wire.

The special comb is laid flat on a board and the outer margins are trimmed away with a warm, sharp knife, leaving the youngest larvae intact in cells at the new comb margins. The comb is now put into the space left in the cell builder and the frames pushed together. Ten days later numerous queen cells should be ready for distribution to colonies to be requeened, which should have been de-queened the previous day, or to nuclei. The cells are carefully cut from the comb, taking enough of the surrounding comb to make a base for handling, and are laid in a container lined with layers of cloth, or are placed upright in holes drilled in a block of wood. The cells should be kept out of cold or sun, and be given to the colonies to be requeened or to nuclei as soon as possible. When placing them in those hives they should be carefully stuck to the face of a comb that, preferably, has brood. They should not be adhered to combs of cold, sealed honey because they will be chilled. A toothpick pushed through the bit of comb that was left at the base of the cell may be used to secure the cell to the comb in the hive.

Other beekeepers, before Dr. Miller publicized his method, had devised ways to obtain queen cells when wanted, and some of them allowed the bees to rear queens from young larvae that remained in worker cells. These methods make use of specially prepared worker comb with young larvae that is cut into strips, then attached to the lower edge of a comb from which the lower part has been removed, or to a bar that can be suspended in an empty frame. In some cases worker cells with young larvae are cut out of the comb with a special punch and attached to bars.

Among the beekeepers using the strip method was Henry Alley (1883), one of the first beekeepers to sell queens. When the grafting method of queen rearing became popular the older methods were discarded by most beekeepers. There are some, however, who dislike grafting and retain the older methods. Jay Smith, a well known Indiana queen breeder, reared queens by the Doolittle method for many years and contributed his own modifications to that method (Smith 1923). Toward the end of his career he became convinced that queens reared by the Alley method were superior to those that had been grafted, and in 1949 he published his adaptation of the Alley method.

Smith's system involves the use of a special breeder hive that functions on the same principle as the breeder hive insert, and he used starter and finisher colonies. The breeder hive body is divided by a division board into a small compartment for three frames and a large compartment for six frames. The division board extends three-fourths inch above the edge of the hive and to within one inch of the bottom board; the space below is filled with a strip of queen excluder which is tacked to the division board and rests against a cleat fastened to the bottom board to prevent the queen from passing beneath the excluder. The normal hive entrance is closed, or a special bottom board is used. The smaller compartment has no outside entrance while the entrance to the larger compartment is located beneath the handhold on the side and is of similar dimensions as the handhold. A hole bored in the side of the smaller compartment gives access to a feeder attached to the outer wall. Each compartment is closed on top with a wooden inner cover, and a telescope cover serves as an outer cover.

The queen is confined to the small compartment on three special full size frames. Two of these have a piece of comb five and one-half inches wide and nine and one-half inches long that is attached to the top bar of the frame at the middle. The remainder of the frame is filled with board (Fig. 25). Those frames remain against the sidewalls of the small compartment. The third frame of the small compartment has a new comb approximately the same size as the comb in the side frames. This was obtained by attaching a piece of foundation five and one-half inches by nine and one-half inches to the middle of an empty frame (Fig. 26) and having it drawn out in the larger compartment of the breeder hive or in a cell finishing colony. It is necessary that additional combs be

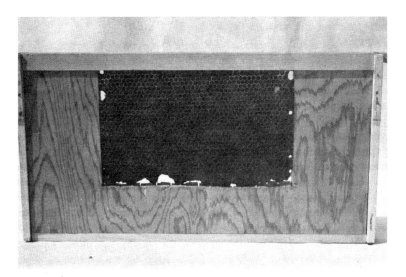

Fig. 25. The side frames of the small compartment of the Jay Smith breeder hive have comb at the middle and the rest of the frame filled with wood.

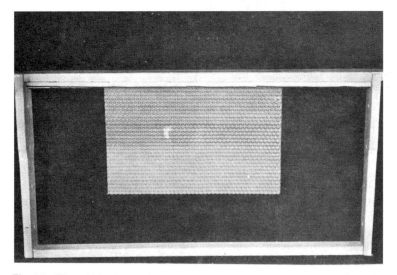

Fig. 26. The middle frame of the small compartment of the Smith breeder hive has foundation in the middle that will be drawn out for the queen to lay in, after which it is cut into strips that will be attached to bars.

drawn out continuously so that one is always available to put into the small compartment between the frames with wood.

The breeder hive is stocked by putting one comb of brood with adhering bees and the queen in the small compartment between the frames with wood. The large compartment is then filled out with brood and bees from the original breeder hive. The colony is fed continuously. After the side combs of the small compartment are filled with brood the center comb of brood is replaced with one of the new white combs. About twenty-four hours later the new comb is filled with eggs, and it is moved to the large compartment and next to the division board, or into a cell finisher colony, for incubation and later for the first feeding of the larvae. This routine is followed daily; the combs with youngest eggs are placed next to the division board and the combs with the older eggs are pushed toward the opposite sidewall of the large compartment. When the fourth comb of eggs is transferred to the large compartment the first comb now has young larvae ready for preparation for the cell starter colony.

The breeder colony may be given a comb of emerging brood each week, and a comb of bees from the starter colony may also be shaken onto the entrance if needed because this colony cannot maintain itself.

When preparing the larvae for the starter colony, the comb with young larvae is laid on a board and, with a warmed sharp knife, is cut from the frame. Strips are now cut lengthwise leaving intact alternate rows of comb cells with young larvae. A seam of wax just at its melting point is laid along one side of a bar that is as wide and thick as a frame bottom bar and just long enough to fit inside an empty frame. A strip of larvae is set into the wax and may be painted with wax along each side with a narrow brush. Because worker cells are so close together queen cells built from them cannot be separated and it is necessary to destroy some of the larvae. Every third larva is left, destroying the two between by pushing the cell walls over them. Two or three bars of prepared cells are put into a cell bar frame and two frames of bars are put into a swarm box for starting.

For requeening even as few as one or two colonies the "grafting" technique is useful and convenient. The old queen is removed from the colony to be requeened, and larvae are transferred from worker comb with some type of "grafting needle" to natural cell cups on the combs of the colony to be requeened. The following day very young well-fed larvae may be substituted for the larvae of cells the bees "accepted." In about two weeks a young laying queen can be expected to be in the colonies so treated. However, when more queens are needed it is better to use methods more appropriate to large scale queen rearing.

A toothpick with one end shaved to a thin edge, moistened, and the terminal 1/16" of the shaved end bent to almost 90° makes a very good temporary grafting needle. A 30° bend in the opposite direction one-half inch from the hook end facilitates seeing the larvae in the worker cells.

Rearing Many Queens

All, or at least nearly all, of the commercial queen rearers in the United States use Doolittle's method of transferring young larvae from worker comb into specially prepared queen cell cups (Doolittle 1888). This method has been challenged from time to time as resulting in queens inferior to queens produced "from the egg." Actually, the usual methods of producing queens from the egg do not do that at all, but, like the grafting method, from young larvae. It still must be shown that such queens are superior to those reared by grafting, and grafting is a much more convenient and economical method.

Preparation for Rearing Virgins by the Grafting Method

While the grafting method is not difficult, the queen rearer can become frustrated and disappointed unless needed preparations are made before beginning the program.

It is assumed that the queen mother colonies, and strong colonies for use in cell building, have been selected and brought to the cell building area.

Cell Cups. Beeswax or plastic cell cups are essential to the grafting method, and where to get them is of immediate concern to the beginning queen rearer. When few cups are needed, they can be obtained by cutting off the "embryo" cups which are present in most colonies. Drone comb cells may be substituted for queen cell cups. Individual drone cells that have been cut down to one-fourth inch of the midrib may be fastened to bars in the same way as queen cell cups, or strips of drone cells similarly prepared may be attached to bars with melted wax. The cells into which larvae will be transferred should be separated by destroying two drone cells between them.

The beginner is not alone in concern about cell cups; the professionals who use thousands of cups differ in their preferences for different kinds of cell cups, or, if made by the queen rearer, how to make them. Whatever the beekeeper decides about cell cups, the cups and the wax they are made from must *not* be exposed to insecticides. Pest strips and household sprays in the same room with cell cups are particularly insidious and harmful because their vapors are absorbed by the wax. The queen rearer would be wise to ensure that the wax for cell cups is as pure as can be obtained. The color of the wax seems to be of little consequence as long as the wax has not been scorched; though light wax, such as is obtained from comb cappings, is preferable. Cell cup size can vary within limits with no difference in acceptance by the bees. Inside diameters of 1/4 to 5/16 inch are satisfactory.

Some beekeepers who rear thousands of queens a year buy cell cups, made of beeswax or plastic, from bee supply houses or directly from the maker. The beekeeper who needs to rear only a few queens will find that purchase of cell cups is convenient and economical. There is some satisfaction, however, in "dipping" the cups needed.

When only a few to several hundred cups are needed, a single forming stick is sufficient. The stick should be made of thoroughly seasoned round hardwood and be about three inches long. It should taper from approximately a three-eighth inch diameter at a point one-half inch from the tip to a diameter of one-fourth to five-sixteenths inch at the tip. The end is rounded to give the bottom of the wax cup a concave form. The taper is merely to make the removal of the cups from the stick easier. The surface of the forming stick should be smooth. Forming "sticks" made of aluminum or stainless steel are fully as satisfactory as those made of wood.

The wax should be melted in a tray on a thermostatically controlled hot plate, or in a double-jacketed tray, the lower part of which is partly filled with water, and be kept at a temperature just above its melting point. When the wax is ready, the forming stick is dipped into clean, cold water and is touched to a towel, or the excess water shaken off. The stick is then dipped into the wax to a depth of about three-eighths inch, and is then quickly withdrawn and held above the tray for a few moments to allow the wax to solidify (Fig. 27). This is repeated four or five times, after which the stick is submerged into cold water to solidify the wax. The cup can be removed from the forming stick by a gentle twist. This procedure is followed for each cup.

The wax cups are attached to wooden bars that fit between the end bars of a standard frame and that rest upon blocks nailed to the inside of the frame ends or in slots made in the inner side of the frame end-bars. The blocks or slots are situated so there is a one and one-half inch space below the lower cell bar and the frame bottom bar and between the cell bars. Frames may be constructed to take three or four cell bars. Those that take three usually have comb above the top bar of cups with a permanent bar beneath the strip of comb, but this is not necessary.

To attach the cell cups to the bars, a bar is laid on a drip sheet and some melted wax is ladled along the upper side of the bar to form

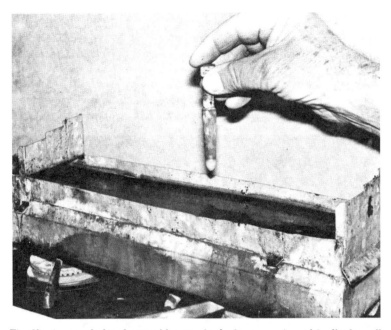

Fig. 27. A water jacketed tray with water in the lower tray is used in dipping cell cups when the wax is melted over an open flame. Each cup may be dipped individually with a single forming stick.

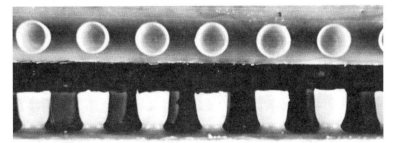

Fig. 28. Cell cups are attached to a bar with melted wax, or are set on "chips," or in wooden cell cup bases which are attached to a bar.

a base for the cells and to fasten them to the bar; or with a wax-tube fastener, baster, or medicine dropper a bead of melted wax may be drawn along the middle of the bar from end to end, or a wax spot deposited for each cup. The cups are pressed into the soft or barely melted wax and spaced about three-fourths to seven-eighths inch from center to center, fifteen to sixteen cups are placed on each bar (Fig. 28). When the bar is filled with cups, additional melted wax may be deposited along the side of and between the cups to reinforce their attachment. Some bee-keepers prefer to seat the wax cups into wooden base cups that can be pressed into the wax on the bar and which give each cell a solid base for handling (Fig. 29). Thin wooden pieces called "chips" are sometimes used as cell cup bases in the same way as the wooden base cups.

Fig. 29.   a   b   c   d   e
Various kinds of cell cups and cup bases currently in use: (a) plastic cup on wax base; (b) wax cup on wooden "chip" base; (c) wax cup in wooden cell base; (d) pressed cell cup and base; (e) dipped cell cup adhered to base with melted wax.

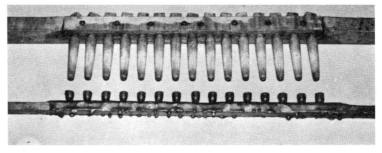

Fig. 30. Multiple forming sticks fastened together for dipping many cell cups at once.

When cell cups are needed in large quantities, dipping one cup at a time is impractical. A form for dipping enough cells at once for one bar can be made by attaching fifteen or sixteen cell forming sticks of the same length to a thick strip of wood and spacing the forming sticks three-fourths to seven-eighths inch apart from center to center (Fig. 30). As

Fig. 31. Ten strips of forming sticks may be fastened together for dipping 150 to 160 cups at one time.

many as ten of these bars of sticks may be fitted together to dip 150 to 160 cups at one time (Fig. 31). The wax for the cups is melted in a tray on a thermostatically controlled hot plate or in a water-jacketed tray. A guide for gauging the depth to which the sticks are dipped should be part of the dipping tray.

The wax for attaching the cups to the bars is melted in a similar but wider tray that is one and one-half inches shorter than the cell bar. The wax in this tray is also at a temperature just above its melting point. Additionally, a tray long enough to receive the entire row of dipping sticks, and in which is put moderately soapy cold water, is needed to wet the sticks before dipping (Fig. 32) so the sticks can be withdrawn easily from the solidified wax cups. The sticks are soaked in the mild soap solution for half an hour before use. A container of cold water that is long and wide enough to easily receive the row of forming sticks and the bar is needed for cooling and washing the cups.

Before dipping the forming sticks into the wax, a cell bar is laid over the pan of wax used for attaching the cell cups to the bars, where

Fig. 32. The sticks are soaked in moderately soapy water for about one-half hour before use. After the sticks are withdrawn from the formed cell cups, they are again submerged in the soapy water before new cells are dipped.

it is supported by the ends of the pan, and wax is ladled over the upper surface. The forming sticks are now taken from the soap solution and touched to a towel to remove water droplets at the ends of the sticks. They are then dipped about three-eighths inch into the melted wax in the dipping tray and are immediately withdrawn and held above the tray for a few moments until the wax on the sticks solidifies somewhat (Fig. 33). This process is repeated three or four times.

Fig. 33. The forming sticks are dipped into the barely melted wax three or four times. Between each dip they are held above the wax momentarily to allow the wax on the sticks to cool.

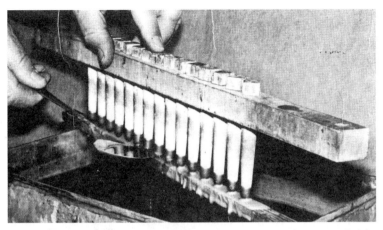

Fig. 34. Wax in another tray is ladled along and between the cups to build a thick base. After the surface of the wax has cooled, the bar will adhere to the cups so bar and forming sticks can be lifted from the tray and submerged in a container of cooling water.

Fig. 35. The forming sticks can be withdrawn from the cups by pushing the bar and attached cups away from the forming sticks by gentle, even pressure on the ends of the bar.

After the last dip, wax is again ladled over the bar, and the sticks with the dipped cell cups are rested on the bar. If a thicker base is desired, additional wax may be ladled along the sides and between the cup bases (Fig. 34). The sticks are held steady until the wax has cooled enough to appear somewhat solidified which is sufficient to adhere the bar to the cups for transfer to the cooling container of water.

The forming sticks with the formed cups and adhering bar are lifted off of the tray and submerged in the cooling water. While the cups are held under water the bar can be pushed away from the sticks by gentle, even pressure on the ends of the bar with the thumbs (Fig. 35), leaving

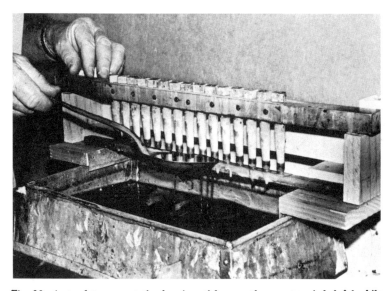

Fig. 36. A stand to support the forming sticks over the wax tray is helpful while wax is ladled around the cup bases.

the cups attached to the bar. The cups should be rinsed to remove any soap that may have remained in them.

The process of attaching the cups to the bars is made easier if the forming sticks with the dipped cups are rested on the cell bar with the aid of a support (Fig. 36). Additional wax may be ladled along the bar and around the cup bases if a thicker base is desired. When the wax has cooled somewhat, the forming sticks with the adhering bar can be lifted from the support and submerged in the water of the cooling container.

The sticks must again be dipped in the soap solution before the next bar of cups is dipped.

Cell cups can be dipped and fastened to bars even more quickly by dipping ten bars at once, and after the wax has solidified, separating the forming sticks and resting each upon a cell bar that is supported by a special rack (Fig. 37). Wax is poured around the cups, first those on one side of the rack and then the other. By the time the wax has been poured around the cells on the second side of the rack the wax on the first side has cooled and the cells may be pushed off of the forming sticks.

Cells should always be rinsed, after removal from the forming sticks, to eliminate traces of soap.

Fig. 37. When ten sets of sticks are dipped at once, they may be separated and rested on bars on a specially designed stand while wax is ladled around the cup bases. It is not necessary to cool the cups in water to remove them from the forming sticks.

Bars of cups can be stored satisfactorily in boxes. A half inch thick strip of wood is placed on the bottom of the box along opposite sides for the bars to rest upon, and also under each layer of cell bars which should be placed in the box with the cells beneath the bars. The boxes of cups must be stored where there is no possibility of contamination with insecticides, such as from pest control strips.

Obtaining Larvae

The "hunt" system. When few cells, or a hundred or so, are to be grafted, the simplest way to get larvae for transfer to queen cell cups is to look in the queen mother colony for well fed larvae the right size in a comb having eggs and recently hatched larvae, or well fed very young larvae adjacent to eggs near comb margins. This method of finding suitable larvae is slow because each larva must be selected carefully for size that denotes proper age, and for copious feeding.

Fig. 38. Well filled combs of pollen, or cakes of pollen + pollen supplement, are necessary in the hive for good cell building if little or no pollen is being brought in from the field.

Comb in breeder colony and to feeder colony. When several hundred cells are to be grafted, the process of larval transfer is faster and easier if most of the larvae in a comb are all within the proper age for grafting and are abundantly fed. Such a comb of larvae can be obtained by putting a warm, polished dark comb in the broodnest of the breeder or queen mother colony. The next day the comb is put into a specially prepared colony for feeding.

This colony is prepared by removing the queen and unsealed brood temporarily. The queen, unsealed brood, and about half the bees, can be set above a divide board with an entrance to the front, or on a bottom board to the rear of the hive. Sugar syrup made by dissolving four parts of granulated sugar in six parts of water by volume (40:60 syrup) should be fed the colony a day or so before preparing it to feed the larvae, and continued during the time the larvae are being fed. When preparing the colony, a frame well filled with pollen (Fig. 38) should be placed on each side of the space that will receive the frame of eggs from the queen mother colony. Four days after the day the comb was given to the queen mother colony the larvae are ready for transferring to queen cell cups, and each should be resting on a bed of jelly that covers much of the cell bottom. Some cells of the worker comb will frequently have been modified as beginning queen cells (Fig. 6), and the larvae from these may be used.

This feeding colony may be used to start the grafted cells also, which can be put into the place that had been occupied by the comb of larvae, or it may feed the cells until they are sealed at which time the cells can be moved to an incubator colony and the queen and brood returned to the feeding colony.

If it is preferred, a five frame nucleus for feeding the larvae may be made up in a nucleus box or in a hive body with a follower board. In this case, two combs of older larvae or sealed or emerging brood and two combs with pollen are used and extra bees are shaken into the body. The pollen combs are placed adjacent to the space where the comb with eggs will be put, with the brood combs toward the sides. If this nucleus is maintained by weekly addition of emerging brood or by young bees shaken from combs of larvae, it may be used throughout the active season.

Confinement of breeder queen to one or a few combs. When a breeder queen is to be used as a queen mother for an extended period, it is better to confine the queen on one to five combs in an area partitioned by queen excluders that slide into saw kerfs in each end of a hive body (Fig. 39).

Fig. 39. Breeder queen confined to one comb by excluder partitions.

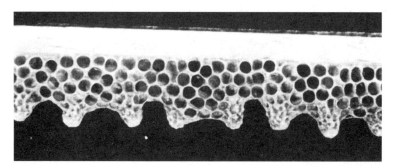

Fig. 40. Sealed queen cells may become "webbed" with comb because of a lack of storage space for incoming nectar or syrup.

One of the combs in the partition, or next to the partition, should have abundant pollen. The remainder of the body is filled with one empty comb, sealed and emerging brood, and one comb with unsealed honey. The colony is fed syrup continuously. In fact, all colonies involved in queen rearing should be fed continuously unless nectar is being gathered in sufficient quantity for the bees to build comb. Colonies that are being fed heavily should always be supplied with an empty comb that is replaced regularly. If webbing of queen cells occurs (Fig. 40), or excessive burr comb is built, a frame of foundation put into the hive usually alleviates the problem.

A warm and polished comb is put into the partition with the queen. Four days later the larvae are ready to graft, and another comb is given the queen. Thus, a queen can be used as a queen mother approximately every four days.

As the brood emerges in the hive outside of the partitioned area, the combs are replaced with sealed brood, and the pollen combs are replaced as the supply of pollen diminishes. In the early part of the season when little pollen is being gathered and the demand for pollen is great, the pollen combs may have to be replaced every few days, and pollen cakes may be fed above the partition.

Some queen breeders prefer to leave a comb with the breeder for only one day when it is then moved to another position in the breeder hive and another comb is given the queen. With this system there will be three combs with eggs in the hive 3 days after the first comb was given to the queen. On the 4th day, the eggs of the first comb given the queen will have hatched and the larvae are ready for grafting. A comb well filled with pollen should be next to this comb. This system allows a queen to be used as a queen mother every day.

Fig. 41. Breeding queen confined to compartment of a half-comb insert.

Breeder queen confined to half-comb insert. One of the best and most convenient methods of obtaining larvae is by use of a special full depth hive body insert (Figs. 41, 42). The breeding queen is confined to three small combs, each about half the size of standard combs, in a compartment with queen excluder sides that makes up half of the insert. Three additional half-combs occupy the other half of the insert, which has open sides. A standard comb well filled with pollen is placed next to one side of the insert, such as to the left, and an empty comb and combs of sealed or emerging brood are put in the remaining spaces of the body. The colony is fed syrup continuously.

Each day the center comb in the partition with the queen is moved with its eggs to the non-excluded half of the insert and placed at the side opposite the standard comb with pollen that is outside the insert, such as to the right side of the insert. The other combs of the non-excluded half are moved across the insert toward the pollen comb after the half-comb on the pollen comb side is removed and given to the queen. Four days from the day a comb was given to the queen, or when the fifth comb is put into the compartment with the queen, the comb that is next to the

Fig. 42. Half-comb insert in place in hive body of breeding queen.

pollen comb will have larvae that are ready to graft. The larvae should be lying on a bed of royal jelly that covers at least half of the bottom of the cells (Fig. 15).

When grafting is completed, the remaining larvae are washed from the comb, the water shaken out, and the comb returned to the queen in the excluder compartment, or put into a special super above an excluder of a strong colony to be conditioned for later use.

Breeder queen confined to compartment in "shallow" or 6⅝" depth body. A commercial variation of the above methods of obtaining larvae is to install the breeding queen in a hive that consists of an 8-frame or 10-frame "shallow" or 6⅝" depth body that has rabbets along the sides and has small frames that fit crossways in the body. An excluder that extends to the bottom board separates three frames at the front from the remaining frames (Fig. 43). The queen is confined to the small compartment. Each day the center comb of the small compartment with its eggs is moved to the larger compartment, next to the excluder, and is replaced by a comb from the larger compartment. A comb well filled with pollen is kept beside the oldest comb of eggs, which is the farthest

Fig. 43. Breeding queen confined by an excluder to three small frames that fit ᴄrossways in a shallow body.

from the excluder, or a pollen patty is placed directly above it. Four days after the breeder colony is arranged, the first comb given to the queen has lavishly fed larvae the right age for grafting. Each day thereafter a similar comb is available.

These breeder colonies are maintained by adding sealed or emerging brood in small combs from special support colonies. The combs from which grafts have been made are put on these colonies for care of the brood that remains in them.

Grafting

Grafting place, humidity, temperature, light. Transferring the larvae to the cell cups can be done almost anywhere and with several kinds of instruments. Nevertheless, more consistent results will be obtained if the proper tools are used and the grafting place is warm and relatively humid. Commercial queen breeders usually have a special room or small house for grafting (Figs. 44, 45). The small grafting house is especially convenient. A temperature of at least 75° F is suitable, and relative humidity of about 50% or above is recommended to prevent drying of the larvae,

Fig. 44. Combination grafting room and storage building.

Fig. 45. Small grafting house used extensively by commercial queen breeders.

which are very small and dry quickly after being transferred. The grafting room can be humidified by boiling some water in a pan, or by sprinkling water on the floor an hour before grafting. The grafted cells can also be covered with a damp cloth for a short time if humidity is low, but in any case, the grafted cells should be given to the cell builders as quickly as possible after they are grafted.

Good light is essential. A bright fluorescent lamp is one of the most satisfactory, though other lamps can be used if they do not project excessive heat. The lamp should be placed so the light shines directly to the bottoms of the comb cells when the comb containing the larvae to be transferred is tilted toward the operator about 30° from horizontal. A loupe may be helpful if it is difficult to see the small larvae, or the outer half of the cells of the comb containing the larvae may be shaved off with a heated, sharp razor blade.

An incubator for holding ripe queen cells overnight is useful, and can be conveniently located in the grafting room or house. An egg incubator may be satisfactory. The temperature should be maintained at about 92° F, and the necessary humidity provided by evaporation from a flat pan of water.

Grafting into natural cups. For rearing queens in natural cell cups found on the combs of colonies to be requeened, the larvae can be transferred from a comb to the cups with a toothpick that has had one end shaved to a feather edge, and, after moistening, 1/16 inch of the thin tip has been bent upward to almost 90°. An additional bend of the toothpick about five-eighths inch from the tip should be made about 30° in the opposite direction so that in using the tool the fingers will not obscure the view into the cells. This tool is strictly for temporary and limited use, but for that purpose it is satisfactory.

Grafting into artificial cups. For more extensive queen rearing, a more substantial and better constructed transferring tool, or "grafting needle," is necessary. Two kinds are in general use: the "straight" needle and the "automatic" with retractable tongue (Fig. 46). With practice one develops skill with either needle and which one is used will probably depend upon personal preference.

In using the straight needle the cups should be warmed in an incubator, under a lamp, or in a strong colony, so the wax is softened to allow the needle to be pressed into the cup bottom as the larva is dislodged from the needle. The needle is lowered beside a sidewall of a worker cell and is slipped sideways under the larva and its bed of royal jelly without digging into the cell bottom. The larva is lifted up and lowered to the bottom of the queen cell cup. Then the needle is pressed into the

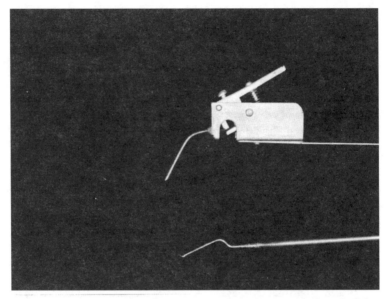

Fig. 46. The "automatic" grafting needle above and the "straight" needle below.

cup bottom slightly, and the tip of the needle is withdrawn leaving the larva and its jelly in the center of the cup.

The automatic needle is used in a similar fashion except the tongue is extended about 1/16 inch before it is slipped sideways under the larva and its jelly. The flat handle of the needle is held between the first and middle fingers, and the extension and retraction of the tongue is controlled by the thumb (Fig. 47). Warming the cups is recommended in all cases, but when the automatic needle is used, the cups need not be softened because after the larva is lowered to the bottom of the cup it is dislodged from the needle by retracting the needle tongue. The automatic needle usually transfers more jelly with the larva than the straight needle, and in this respect it is better.

The "dry grafting" described above is practiced by most commercial queen breeders, who may graft many hundred cells a day and who become very skillful in transferring larvae without injury to them or turning them over on the jelly. The less skilled may find it easier to transfer very young larvae if they "prime" the cell cups with royal jelly. The jelly forms a cushion for dislodging the larvae from the needle. Jelly for grafting can be gathered from natural queen cells or from cells "dry" grafted for that

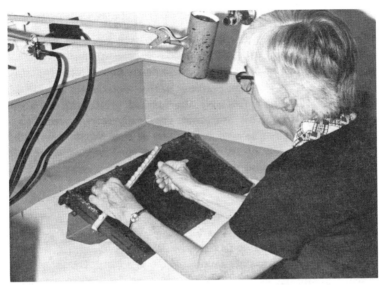

Fig. 47. "Grafting" or transferring very young larvae in worker comb to queen cell cups. An automatic needle is being used.

Fig. 48. Cell cups "primed" with royal jelly preparatory to transfer of young larvae.

purpose. It may be stored in a stoppered vial in a refrigerator or may be dried and reconstituted with water. In either case the jelly is probably not the proper food for very young larvae and its main function is to be a cushion and to prevent the transferred larvae from drying.

To prime the cups, a drop of water, or other suitable diluent, is mixed with the jelly to thin it slightly. With a medicine dropper, or with the end of a match stick, a small drop of jelly is put into the center of the bottom of each cup (Fig. 48). Some prefer to take jelly on a "jelly spoon" and push a small amount into each cup with one end of a straight grafting needle.

Grafting needles, jelly spoons, and medicine droppers should be sterilized frequently in alcohol or in boiling water. If grafts are made into cups primed with royal jelly, the jelly should not have been taken from cells that had been grafted *with* jelly because disease organisms that affect queen larvae or pupae can be passed on to newly grafted cells in the jelly.

Double grafting. Double grafting is the replacement of larvae in "accepted" cells, *the day following* the original graft, with very young abundantly fed larvae. This can assure excellently reared queens even if the cell builders are not as well maintained as they should be. If, however, the various facets of rearing fully developed virgins are carefully observed, it is doubtful that double grafting produces queens that are significantly superior to single grafted queens.

Double grafting can, in fact, result in queens inferior to those that were properly single grafted. If the cells are double grafted on the second or third day following the single graft, the food in the queen cells is not suitable for the very young larvae. Small queens emerging from such double grafted cells are not unusual. If the second larvae of double grafted cells are too old, or have been scantily fed before being transferred, they will not make good queens. A poorly maintained cell builder may feed the cells so miserly the queens do not develop as they should even though the larvae themselves were the proper age and had been well fed before being transferred. Thus, if properly done, double grafting is a good procedure, but it can mislead the queen rearer if it is done improperly.

Building the Cells

Obtaining well fed larvae the right age for grafting is crucial. The care and feeding of the larvae after grafting is fully as important, and the first 24 to 36 hours of this period are the most critical. This means that the newly grafted larvae must receive almost instant attention when given to the bees and that they be fed abundantly from the outset. The attention the bees give the cells the first 24 to 36 hours is commonly known as "starting," and the subsequent 60 to 72 hours of provisioning before the cells are sealed is "finishing." After the cells are sealed they are "incubated" until emergence of the virgins.

Twenty-four to 36 hours after grafting, the cells of well fed larvae will have been elongated, or "drawn," with newly worked wax, and will be nearly half full of royal jelly (Figs. 49 and 16a). If some cells of a bar of cells are poorly provisioned or are crooked, or if the elongation of some of the cells is quite noticeably less than the others, the starting colony needs attention.

Fig. 49. Well fed queen cells thirty-six hours following grafting.

Cells may be started in special starting colonies and transferred later to finishing colonies, or in queenright or queenless starter-finisher colonies where the cells are put immediately after being grafted and are left until they are 9 or 10 days old.

Two general kinds of special starter colonies are currently in use by commercial queen rearers: the confined starter colony, and the free-flying queenless colony.

Starting the cells: Confined starter colonies. As a rule either confined or free-flying starter colonies start to feed, or "accept," a higher percentage of grafted cells than starter-finishers; however, this is not always the case. They are made up so the population consists of a high proportion of proper age nurse bees, but they have no young larvae to feed the royal jelly that is being secreted. When newly grafted cells are given to such bees, the cells are immediately furnished with food in abundance. All starter colonies should be fed sugar syrup continuously, and a comb well filled with pollen should be next to the queen cells. Well filled pollen combs can be accumulated and stored over an excluder of a "stack" colony in the queen yard so they are readily available. A pollen cake or patty should be placed over the frame with the queen cells if good pollen combs are not available.

Fig. 50. The "swarm box" holds five standard frames. Ventilation is provided by a three to six inch space beneath the frames that is screened on the sides, or the space beneath the frames is omitted and the bottom is screened. There is no entrance. A hole in the cover will take a feed jar.

Swarm box. The most popular confined starter colony is the swarm box. The swarm box (Fig. 50) usually holds five standard frames and has a three to six inch space beneath the frames that is screened on the sides, or, instead, on the bottom with transverse cleats two inches thick at each end to provide for ventilation. There is no entrance; the bees are confined the entire time they are in the box. The cover should have a hole at the middle to take a quart glass canning jar. A well filled pollen comb is put in the center, and a comb with unsealed honey or with sugar syrup is placed against each sidewall leaving a space on each side of the pollen comb for the newly grafted queen cells (Fig. 51).

A five standard-frame nucleus box may be converted to a swarm box by replacing the bottom board with a three inch deep rim screened on the bottom. A regular deep body can be modified similarly, but a follower board or a frame wrapped with paper should partition the cell building area from the rest of the body, which should be left empty.

Fig. 51. The swarm box is provisioned with side combs of unsealed honey or sugar syrup. The center comb has pollen. Two spaces are left for the newly grafted queen cells.

One or two hours before newly grafted queen cells are given, the box is stocked with five to six pounds of bees taken from the active brood-nest of a strong colony that is feeding worker larvae well, and which has been receiving sugar syrup unless there is a good nectar flow. It is then set in a quiet and cool dark place, and the syrup feeder is put in place.

Two frames with three bars each of grafted cells (about 90 to 96 cells) are given to the swarm box. The box is jarred to dislodge bees hanging from the cover, and the frames with the cells are put into the two empty spaces, one on each side of the pollen comb. The swarm box is returned to a cool, dark place and left for twenty-four to thirty-six hours when the started and lavishly fed cells are transferred to cell finishing colonies, two or three bars to each. The bees of the swarm box may be divided between the finishing colonies, or returned to the donor colony.

If swarm boxes are to be used each day, or several times a week, it is convenient to designate certain colonies that feed larvae well as swarm-box donor or support colonies. These are two-story colonies with prolific queens. In each colony the queen is confined to the lower body with a queen excluder; sugar syrup is fed, and a well filled pollen comb or pollen patty is provided in the upper body if pollen is not being stored in abundance. On a regular weekly schedule or the day before a swarm box is to be stocked, the bees are shaken from the young brood in the lower body and the young brood is moved into the upper body above the excluder. The queen need not be found, and the nurse bees and comb builders quickly move above to the young brood where they are readily available for the swarm boxes.

While all colonies involved in cell building must be strong with a high proportion of nurse bees and comb builders, support colonies and queenright cell builders may become so crowded they may swarm. A shallow super or 6⅝" depth body of combs placed on the bottom board will give the field bees a place to remain overnight or in bad weather and avoid congestion in the brood area (Fig. 52). In hot weather the support colonies and cell builders should be lightly shaded or provided with top insulation because when they are unprotected in the hot sun many of the bees will desert the upper body and hang outside of the hive, thereby

Fig. 52. Shallow super below cell building body to give a place for field bees at night and during inclement weather.

causing a slackening of brood rearing or cell feeding. Likewise, in cold weather of early spring, insulation should be provided over the tops of cell builders, and it may be advantageous to install thermostatically controlled bottom board heaters.

Modified swarm box. A cell starter in which the bees are confined above a two-story colony for twenty-four to thirty-six hours while cells are being started is an efficient modification of the swarm box.

Strong two-story colonies are prepared as bee donor colonies. The queen is placed beneath an excluder in the bottom body with sealed brood and empty combs, and the combs of young larvae are moved to the upper body. This arrangement is maintained by moving young larvae to the top body and sealed brood below at three-day intervals if successive grafts are to be started.

A full depth body is prepared with two well filled combs of pollen in the middle of the body. A space is left between them for the cells, and a division board feeder is placed next to the outer side of each pollen comb (Fig. 53).

In the morning, or about two hours before newly grafted cells are to be given to the starter, the prepared body is set on an upturned hive cover, or on a "super horse" (Fig. 54) beside the donor colony and upon a screen made of 8-mesh hardware cloth fastened between two ¼" thick rims (Fig. 55). The top body of the donor colony, which has young brood, nurses, and wax builders, is set on top of the prepared body and the bees are shaken from the combs into the starter body, after which the brood body is returned to the donor colony above the excluder. The stocked cell starting body and the screen beneath it are now placed on top of the donor colony (Fig. 56), and the feeders are filled with sugar syrup (4 parts sugar to 6 parts water by volume). There is no entrance to the starter body.

In the early afternoon or about two hours following make-up of the starter body, a graft of four bars of cells is put into the space between the two pollen combs. Twenty-four to thirty-six hours later the started cells are transferred to a finisher colony. The screen is removed, the bees of the starter body are shaken down into the donor colony below, and the starter body is removed.

Some beekeepers prefer to place the started cells down into the second body of the donor colony rather than transfer the started cells to a finisher colony. The bees are rejoined as above. Three days later when the cells are sealed the cells are moved to an incubator colony where they remain until the day before they are due to emerge, that is, until the 10th day from grafting, or a period of five days in the incubator colony.

Fig. 53. Cell starting body prepared with two pollen combs and two division board feeders.

Fig. 54. The use of a "super horse" makes the handling of supers easier when colonies are examined.

A successful variation of the modified swarm box is to place four or five combs of older larvae and sealed or emerging brood with adhering bees, together with a comb with pollen and the addition of a division board feeder, into a full depth body above a screen on a one and one-half story queenless cell builder. The half depth body of the cell builder has honey or empty combs and is on the bottom board. Above it and over an excluder is a full depth cell building body. The cell starting body above the screen has no entrance and is fed sugar syrup in the division board feeder. About two hours after the starter is made up three bars of grafted cells are placed between a comb of brood and the pollen comb in the starting body. They are left for twenty-four to thirty-six hours when they are moved down, with the brood, into the queenless cell builder and left until they are sealed. They are then transferred to an incubator colony. The process may be repeated for one or two successive grafts. After that the cells are started and also finished in the cell building body of this queenless colony which is maintained by the addition of one-half pound of bees or a frame of emerging brood before each new graft.

Starting the Cells:

Free-flying starter colonies. Free-flying starter colonies are queen-less colonies that are not confined, so that the bees have free flight. In

Fig. 55. Division screen that is used between the bee donor colony and the modified swarm box.

Fig. 56. Cell starting donor colonies. One has a cell starting body above a division screen.

contrast to the confined starter colony, successive grafts may be started in them. Commonly, they are moderately strong one-story 8-frame or 10-frame colonies with the side combs removed, leaving 6 or 7 combs with sealed and emerging brood in the body and a space on either side for bees to cluster on the sidewalls of the hive body. This colony is fed sugar syrup continuously. A well filled pollen comb is placed to one side of a space for the grafted cells which is in the middle of the hive. One frame with three bars of cells is put into this space as soon as the cells are grafted, and twenty-four to thirty-six hours later the started cells are transferred to a finishing colony, and a new graft is given to the starter.

The one-story starter colony may accumulate an excess of field bees, and this condition may interfere with good cell starting. The adverse effects of this can be remedied by placing a shallow or 6⅝" depth body of empty combs and honey on the bottom board either above or below an excluder (Fig. 52).

A similar starter colony arrangement that provides space for field bees is to place a full depth body with combs of honey on the bottom board under an excluder. A second body with five combs of sealed and emerging brood, one empty comb, and one well filled pollen comb is put above the excluder. In this case the seven combs are squeezed together in the top body with the pollen comb adjacent to the middle. Enough bees are provided from support colonies to make the colony moderately strong.

A graft of three bars is placed in the middle next to the pollen comb and is left for twenty-four to thirty-six hours when the cells are transferred to a finishing colony. One or two hours later a new graft is given in the same place. The colony is fed sugar syrup continuously and the pollen comb is replaced as often as needed.

Free-flying starter colonies are maintained by the addition of sealed or emerging brood from support standard-frame nuclei, or from finishing colonies, at seven to ten day intervals, at which time all "natural" or spurious queen cells on the combs are destroyed. If additional bees are needed, these should be taken in the morning from open brood of support colonies in other apiaries and left caged, with sugar syrup, in a cool dark place until late afternoon before they are added to the starter colonies.

Modification of free-flying starter colony. An efficient modification of the free-flying starter colony, that employs the starter also as a finishing colony, is used by some beekeepers, and is one of the better methods of cell building for a hobby beekeeper.

A strong 2-story colony with a prolific queen is prepared by placing the queen with sealed brood and empty combs in the lower hive body below an excluder. Unsealed brood is put in the second hive body above the excluder. A "rim" syrup feeder is set on top of the second body (Fig. 57). The rim feeder (Fig. 58) has a rim 2 or 3 inches high that is fastened to a masonite board. A center box, 2 by 2 inches square and one-half inch shorter than the rim depth, is fastened over a center hole. The rim and box are sealed with hot paraffin to the masonite floor to prevent leakage of syrup. Straw is scattered over the feeder floor to prevent bees' drowning. A hive body with several combs of honey is set on the syrup feeder (Fig. 57). The colony is fed sugar syrup if no nectar is coming in, and by scratching cappings off the combs of honey if there is a moderate honey flow.

About twenty-four hours prior to grafting, the hive body with the queen and its bottom board is moved to the rear of the hive where it remains while the cells are being started. The body with brood that was above the excluder, which is to be the cell starting part of the hive, is placed on a bottom board in the original hive location, and the feeder and hive body with honey are put on top. The feeder is supplied with sugar syrup if needed. This part of the colony is now queenless.

Fig. 57. Cell starter colony prepared with rim feeder and widely spaced combs of honey on top.

Fig. 58. "Rim" syrup feeder for cell builder colonies.

Shortly before grafting, the brood of the cell starting hive body is transferred to the honey body above, and a comb well filled with pollen is placed toward the middle of the cell starting body. This body now has only four or five combs. Two frames of grafted cells, each with three bars of 15 or 16 cells on each bar, are placed in the middle of the cell starting body with the pollen comb between them.

Twenty-four to thirty-six hours later the hive with the queen is returned to its original stand and combs of young larvae from this hive are placed in the cell starting body which is placed again over an excluder on the hive body with the queen. One to three bars of started cells are left in the cell starting colony and the other bars are distributed to finishing colonies. When the cells are sealed the process may be repeated for a new graft, using the same colony as a starting colony or rotating starting among the finishing colonies.

Finishing the cells: Queenright finshing colony. Cells started in starter colonies are usually completed in special queenright finishing colonies. These are strong two-story colonies with the queen in the lower body below an excluder. When these colonies become overly strong a shallow or 6⅝" depth body of combs may be placed on the bottom board to give room for field bees that would otherwise crowd the broodnest at night or in inclement weather.

Before giving each new graft of started cells, or at least each seven to ten days, young brood is moved up from below after adhering bees are shaken off; and the comb with the youngest larvae is placed next to the space where the new cells will be located. A well filled pollen comb is put on the other side of this space. The colony is fed sugar syrup continuously.

Three or four days after a graft of no more than 48 started cells is given, the now sealed or nearly sealed cells are moved to the other side of the young larva and another set of newly started cells is put in their place. This process continues, the oldest cells being pushed away from the active cell building area as new cells are added to the finisher, and are removed on the 10th day from grafting or on the 9th day if they are to be held in an incubator overnight. The frames would be arranged:

<pre>
        h   e   h
        or   or   or
        s C C L l c   pl L s   where
</pre>

c = open cells being built, C = sealed and nearly sealed cells, e = empty comb, h = honey, l = very young larvae, L = older larvae, pl = pollen, s = sealed or emerging brood.

Fig. 59. Three colony cell finishing unit.

The sealed cells may be transferred to an incubator colony instead of leaving them in the finisher, and, in either case, on the 9th day from grafting they may be put into an incubator until sometime the next day. Virgins from properly produced and cared for queen cells will emerge on the 11th or 12th day from grafting.

Alternately, finishing colonies may be given *one* bar of 15 or 16 started cells *each* day. The first started cells are sealed three days after they are given to the finisher, and they are transferred to an incubator *colony* where they remain until the 9th day from grafting when they should be put into an incubator until the next day. In this way each cell builder receives one bar of started cells and yields one bar of sealed cells every day. Only two bars of cells are being fed heavily at the same time, when three bars are in the finisher, because the oldest cells have already been supplied with food and are being sealed.

If a routine is established so that empty or emerging combs of brood are placed in a particular position in the lower body before each graft, the task of raising young larvae is simplified.

Variation of queenright finisher. A successful variation of the queenright finisher is used by some queen breeders. Three colonies form a cell finishing unit; one colony is a support colony and two are cell finishers.

The support colony is two-story and is located between the two finishers (Fig. 59). It has a prolific queen and is fed constantly. An auger hole is bored in the center of the front of each body.

The cell finishers are three-story (Fig. 59). The bottom body has honey and one or two empty combs at the middle which provide a place for field and old bees. An auger hole is bored in the center of the front of this body. Pollen gatherers tend to deposit pollen in the combs adjacent to this hole which assists in the search for well filled pollen combs. The top hive body has empty combs. The bees move the honey from the body on the bottom board to the top body which simulates a nectar flow. About once a week the combs with honey or syrup in the top body are exchanged for empty combs and combs with pollen in the bottom body. Thus a continuous movement of food from the bottom body to the top body is established.

The queen is confined to one comb in a built-in excluder cage in the middle of the second body (Fig. 60). A well filled pollen comb is placed against each outer side of the excluder cage, and the rest of the body is filled with combs of sealed and emerging brood from the support colony, or, if necessary, from other colonies. A frame with three or four bars of cells from a starter colony is given to the finisher between the pollen comb and a comb of sealed brood, first on one side of the queen chamber and then on the other, every four days, after transferring the "ripe" cells that occupied the space to an incubator overnight. At the same time a new comb of emerging brood from a side of the body is given to the queen and dated, and the frame of eggs is transferred from the queen chamber to the support colony to feed. Sealed brood near emergence from the support colony is returned to the cell finisher for emergence. If necessary, the pollen combs are replaced. The two finishers and their support colony are fed sugar syrup continuously.

Starter-finisher cell builders. Starter-finisher cell builders start the newly grafted cells and also finish them. They may be queenless or queenright. The queenright starter-finisher is probably the most conveniently prepared cell builder for the beekeeper who needs a small number of cells, and the queens produced are almost always well developed, especially if the cells were properly double grafted.

Both the queenless and queenright starter-finishers are used by commercial queen breeders.

Queenright starter-finishers. The queenright starter-finisher is the same as the queenright finisher described earlier and is maintained and used in a similar way. The only difference is the newly grafted cells are given directly to the cell builder instead of being started in a special starting colony.

Modification of the usual queenright starter-finisher colony. An excellent modification of the queenright starter-finisher is a colony arranged

Fig. 60. The queen is confined in an excluder cage in the second body of this queenright cell finisher.

Fig. 61. Single story queenless cell starter-finisher colonies.

so the queen, young brood, and some empty combs are in the top body of a 2½ or 3-story colony. Sealed and emerging brood and, initially, one comb of young larvae are in the body on the bottom board. The middle body has empty combs or combs with unsealed honey and is separated from the bottom body by an excluder. The colony is arranged at least a few hours before receiving prepared queen cells. When the cells are given, the comb of larvae is moved to the top body and the cells are put in its place.

Maintenance of the colony resembles that of the usual queenright cell builder in that young brood is moved up and sealed and emerging brood is moved down. It differs in that the queen remains with the young brood and the cells are started and finished by bees in a body with older brood and near the hive entrance. As is customary, sealed cells may be moved toward the side of the lower body or transferred to incubator colonies when new grafts are given to the cell builder.

Queenless starter-finisher colonies. Queenless starter-finisher colonies are one-story (Fig. 61) or one-story with a shallow or 6⅝" depth body of combs on the bottom board with an excluder between the two bodies. Sometimes a rim is used on the bottom board beneath an excluder and a shallow body (Fig. 52). Eight-frame bodies are often preferred to larger bodies. These are made up originally with sealed or emerging brood and extra bees to make the colony strong. A well filled pollen comb is placed near the middle of the body next to the space where the newly grafted cells will be put. The colony is fed constantly. They are maintained by the addition of about ½ pound to 1 pound of bees the evening before each new graft. In some cases emerging brood is given. Frequent additions of ½ to 1 pound of bees or 1 comb of emerging brood is preferable to adding more bees or brood at longer intervals.

A new graft is given each 3 or 4 days, and the previous graft of sealed or nearly sealed cells is transferred to the opposite side of the pollen comb or to an incubator colony. The "ripe" cells are moved to an incubator on the 9th day from grafting, or left until the 10th day and then put into mating nuclei.

Fig. 62. Incubator for holding "ripe" queen cells overnight.

Fig. 63. Incubator rack with bars of queen cells.

The greatest advantage of the queenless starter-finisher is that it is not necessary to examine the combs for natural queen cells. The package bee shipper who is filling packages every day or several times a week often finds the use of queenless starter-finisher cell builders fits in well with his operations because supporting bees are readily available as he fills packages. Before the shipment of packages begins, it is necessary to obtain young bees specifically for the cell builders.

Incubator Colony

An incubator colony is a strong three-story queenless colony which has an excluder between the bottom board and the lower body as a guard against virgins entering. The lower body is filled with combs of honey. Each of the upper bodies has five combs of sealed brood: one at each sidewall, one at the middle, and one at the third space from each side. Each seven to ten days the colony is maintained with sealed brood and, if necessary, with bees from support colonies which have been caged several hours in a cool dark place and sprayed lightly with 40:60 syrup. Any natural cells are destroyed at this time. In late afternoon the bees to be added are again sprayed lightly with 40:60 syrup and added to the colony. The incubator colony is fed syrup continuously. The sealed cells remain in the incubator colony until nine days following grafting when they are put into an incubator overnight. This precaution is advisable as occasionally a queen will emerge early and cause destruction of many cells.

Incubators

Incubators (Fig. 62) for queen cells are usually poultry egg incubators. The temperature is kept at about 92° F and the air is humidified by means of a wide pan of water in the incubator. Incubators are used by many queen breeders, but by no means by all; some queen breeders prefer to leave the cells in the cell builder until the tenth day from grafting.

Removing Bars of Cells From Frames

When bars of cells are removed from a cell bar frame care must be taken that cells are not damaged. One of the easiest methods of removal is to lay the frame with cells on a flat surface and push the bars from one end of the frame while raising that end. When the bars are free, the frame is swung up and over the other ends of the bars.

In some cases when bars of ripe cells are put in an incubator they are left in the frames. In other cases the bars of cells are placed on racks that will fit in the incubator (Fig. 63).

Fig. 64.   a   b   c
Three types of nursery cages: (a) two-hole queen shipping cage with entry hole enlarged to receive queen cell; (b) Laidlaw cage; (c) Alley cage.

Virgin Nurseries

In general, emerging virgins in cages is not recommended. Virgins more than a few hours old are much more difficult to introduce to either nuclei or full colonies than laying queens or queen cells. Bee scientists routinely emerge virgins in cages (Fig. 64) for their special purposes and for artificial insemination, but beekeepers would likely be disappointed with the proportion of successful introductions.

Fig. 65. Frame of nursery cages and nursery colony.

Any strong colony with an abundance of young bees will serve as a virgin nursery. Queenright colonies arranged as queenright cell finishers will care for virgin queens and will also finish queen cells at the same time, but it is preferable that queen nurseries be queenless because virgin nursery colonies may swarm every day. If queenless, the bees soon return to the nursery. Queenless nurseries should be made up with a frame with pollen in the middle of the body, with sealed or emerging brood next to the sidewalls, and with a frame of young larvae in the third position from each side of the body. On either side of the frame of larvae is a space for a frame with nursery cages (Fig. 65). The wire side of the nursery cages should face the larvae. This frame arrangement would be s v l v pl v l v s where l = young larvae, pl = pollen comb, s = sealed or emerging brood, and v = caged virgins. Nursery colonies are maintained by weekly addition of young larvae and of sealed brood or young bees. The nursery should be fed constantly, and pollen should be supplied in combs or as cakes. Nursery colonies usually have one full depth body for the active nursery area, but as the colony becomes stronger a shallow or full depth body with honey may be set on the bottom board as a clustering place for field bees.

The caged virgins will be fed by the bees, and candy in the cages is usually not necessary. They should be introduced to colonies or mating nuclei as soon after emergence as possible and in any case before they are four days old so they will mate close to the normal mating age of 6 to 8 days.

Fig. 66. Park feeder for cell building colonies.

Feeders

Every beekeeper has his favorite method of feeding his colonies sugar syrup, and most of them are quite satisfactory. The Doolittle division board feeder for feeding at intervals long enough for all of the syrup to be taken is satisfactory. For continuous feeding, a pail with a perforated lid on the top of the hive or in an empty body, or a Boardman entrance feeder are very good. A system of piping the syrup from a tank to individual colonies is preferred by some beekeepers. One of the most convenient feeders for cell builders is the Park feeder (Fig. 66) that fits at the back of the hive and is secured to a thin frame, open at the back, that is held between two bodies. The bees enter a small screened compartment built against the side of the feeder next to the hive (Fig. 67).

Fig. 67. Details of Park feeder.

Pollen is as essential for cell building as is syrup or honey, and it is conveniently fed in the comb. When pollen is not available in the comb or when no, or little, pollen is being gathered, pollen or pollen supplement should be fed. Pollen-syrup or pollen-supplement-syrup mixtures are fed as pollen cakes which are usually placed directly on the frames over the cell building area. When colonies are opened frequently it is more convenient to put the cake on a feeder screen (Fig. 68) so it can be easily set aside while the colony is open.

Records

Some kind of record system that will aid the beekeeper in maintaining an orderly flow of queen cells through his cell builders is needed when more than a few cells are produced.

The system of putting new cells in a definite place in the cell builder and moving the older ones to the side shows the relative ages of the different cells. Some queen breeders also write the grafting date on the cell frame top bar in addition, and may make notes on the side or top of the hives.

The cell builders may be divided into three groups (Fig. 69), each of which is identified by a letter or number. New cells are put into a dif-

Fig. 68. Pollen and pollen supplement feeding screen.

ferent group on successive days so that a system of rotation is established whereby each group of cell builders receives new cells and yields ripe cells every three days. If cells were started in a swarm box or starter colony, the oldest cells in the cell builder will be ten days old when the new graft is given and are ready for distribution to mating nuclei. If the ripe cells were started in the cell builder they are nine days old when the new graft is given and they should be left overnight in the cell builder, in an incubator, or incubator colony before distribution to nuclei.

A graft record kept in the grafting room is invaluable to show into which group of builders the cells were put and when they should come out. If starters are used and if stock evaluation and selection is practiced, a graft record should include information pertaining to these items. One satisfactory format includes columns for the date cells are grafted, number of cells, breeders used, identity of starter colonies, cell builder group receiving the cells, number of cells completed, date cells *must be removed* from the builder, disposition of the cells, and remarks the breeder wishes to make.

Fig. 69. Cell builders divided into three groups each of which receives attention on different days.

GRAFT RECORD

Date Grafted	No. of Cells	Breeder	Starter	Cell Builder	No. Completed	Date Out	Disposition and Remarks

Ordinarily a record of cells completed is not particularly useful if the percentage of completed cells is consistent, but is helpful in finding causes of abnormally low percentages of completed cells.

Some queen breeders write the date grafted on the frame top bar of the cell frames. The breeder identification may also be written there if more than one breeder is used on any particular day.

Usually at least 75% of the grafted cells will be accepted and satisfactorily completed. Thus each cell builder can be expected to produce about 30 cells each three days, or 10 cells per day.

CHAPTER IV

Mating the Queen

While the first critical concern in rearing queen bees is obtaining large, fully developed virgins, even the best reared queen is of no value to a colony until she mates and her spermatheca is filled with spermatozoa. Thus, the beekeeper must provide for the mating of the virgins. This may be accomplished by permitting the virgin to mate from the colony to be requeened, or to mate her from special mating colonies known as "nuclei," or from "board divides."

Providing Mates

Virgin queens mate with seven to ten drones or more, and for this reason an abundance of suitable drones within mating range of the virgins' colonies is essential. Queens and drones may fly several miles from their hives on the mating flight, and if there is a scarcity of mature flying drones in the area, the queen may fly so far she fails to return. It is well established that drones from surrounding colonies assemble in congregation areas to which queens find their way. These areas may or may not be near the nucleus yard. One might infer from this that placing drone mother colonies in or near the nucleus yard is little help in providing mates. On the other hand, drones from the mating apiary are as likely to assemble in the congregation area as are other drones, as far as we know. This seems reason enough to stock the immediate area of the nucleus apiary with drones, and also to establish drone mothers in outlying apiaries that are within a radius of two or three miles. For the queen breeder, an abundance of mature drones is as important as a nectar flow to the honey producer.

When only a few to several hundred queens are reared, the availability of enough mature drones to inseminate the queens is rarely a problem, though the genetic quality of the drones may be. When queens are reared by the thousands, there may be hundreds of queens competing for mates in a single afternoon, and this may be repeated on successive afternoons by other queens. In such cases, a continuing supply of mature drones is a major consideration.

The surest way of providing an abundance of queen mates is to place drone comb in the selected drone mother colonies. This is done systematically and should be begun 35 to 40 days before the first mature drones will be needed. The drone mother colonies should be strong, and should

[79]

be fed syrup and pollen unless there is a good flow of pollen and nectar. Drones emerge 24 days after the drone eggs were laid and are mature about 10 days later if properly cared for by the bees. The queen may deposit eggs in the drone comb over a period of several days, and drones will emerge and mature over a similar period. About three thousand drones will emerge from a full drone comb in the spring. Queens mate with seven to ten or more drones, so conservatively the emergence from one drone comb should furnish sufficient mates for 200 virgins. On this basis, one drone mother colony is needed for approximately each two hundred queens to be mated. About twenty-four days after the first emerged drones are mature, there will have been another emergence of drone brood and the drones matured. There will be in addition, of course, drone emergence from drone cells of the other combs of the broodnest.

In commercial queen rearing, mating nuclei are established daily in groups, with ripe queen cells, over a period of about two weeks. One drone mother colony should be provided for each 200 nuclei of a group, and each should be given a drone comb, that fills the frame, 35 to 40 days before the virgins of that group should mate. Two weeks later duplicate drone mothers should receive drone comb to produce mates for the second lot of queens in the nuclei that emerged after the first queens were removed and the nuclei were re-celled. The second drone comb may be placed in the original drone mother colonies, but drones do not mature well in colonies overcrowded with drones and it is better to use duplicate colonies.

Mating Queens From Full Size Hives

The beekeeper who wishes to requeen his colonies or to increase the number may find the most convenient method of mating the queens is to place a ripe queen cell in the colony that will need a new queen.

Requeening

The queen is removed from a colony to be requeened and the following day a "ripe" queen cell, one that is 10 or 11 days old, is attached by its base to the side of a comb, preferably one with emerging bees. Fourteen days later the new queen should be laying well.

Some beekeepers who operate many colonies for honey production attempt to avoid the task of removing the old queen by placing a ripe queen cell between the top bars of two center frames of the top honey super before the peak of the honey flow. The emerged virgin works her way below and mates. In many cases the old queen soon disappears, but sometimes she survives and the young queen is lost.

Fig. 70. Hive entrance reduced with "robber screen" that restricts the entrance but not ventilation and allows the bees to walk over the hive body protected by the screen.

Another time-saving method of requeening with cells is to place an excluder between the two bodies of a two-story broodnest. Four to ten days later the body with eggs is put on top of the honey supers and may be given an entrance. A ripe queen cell is put in the body without eggs which is now on the bottom board. Later the old queen may be destroyed and the two brood bodies combined. A less sure way to retain the young queen is to simply combine the two brood bodies without removing the old queen.

Increase or "divides"

New colonies may be made from established colonies by making up each new colony with two frames of older brood and adhering bees, two combs of honey, and the body filled out with empty combs. Additional bees from two or three combs should be added. The new colony is moved to a location at least two miles away, and a ripe queen cell is pressed by its base into one of the brood combs. It is advisable to reduce the entrance to about one inch with a robber screen (Fig. 70). Two weeks later the colony should have a laying queen.

A robber screen is constructed like a small moving screen. It allows the bees to come out of the hive entrance and walk on the front of the hive where they are protected behind the screen. Robbers are attracted to hive odors that pass through the screen but cannot reduce ventilation enough to suffocate the colony, and the colony can effectively guard the small entrance at the end of the screen. The screen should be put on the hive before robbing starts. If it is put on after severe robbing is in progress robbing will eventually be controlled, but the bottom board will be covered with dead bees that must be removed and the screen replaced.

Should severe robbing be in progress before the screen is installed on the entrance, many of the robbers can be driven from the hive by blowing cool smoke into the hive and allowing them to escape.

Mating Colonies or Nuclei

There are numerous styles of nuclei for mating queens. They range from standard full depth bodies divided into two, three, or four divisions; narrow single full depth bodies that hold three, four, or five frames; shallow bodies divided into compartments lengthwise, crosswise, or both lengthwise and crosswise; smaller boxes with one or two compartments; and "baby" nuclei. The kind of nucleus used depends upon the preferences of the beekeeper, his type of operation, and the climate prevailing during queen rearing.

"Board Divides"

When relatively few queens are needed for a beekeeper's own use one of the least expensive and most convenient arrangements is the "board divide" (Fig. 71). Two or three combs of sealed brood, one or two combs of honey, and adhering bees are taken from the parent colony and placed in a body which is set upon an inner cover that has the hole or slit in the middle closed with wire cloth or piece of thin board. A small entrance is made in the rim at one end, or an auger hole entrance may be cut in one end of the hive body. Additional bees from three or four combs of the parent colony are shaken into the body.

The body and inner cover are now set over the top body of the parent colony with the entrance to the rear of the hive. A ripe queen cell is given to the divide a few hours later. Fourteen days following establishment of the board divide the queen should be laying and may be removed. A second cell may be given to the divide, after removal of the laying queen, and this may be repeated as often as desired. It may be necessary to feed the divide with frames of honey or with sugar syrup when successive queens are mated from the divide.

Fig. 71. Divide board between upper and lower bodies.

Single full-depth or shallow standard-frame nuclei

Mating hives with a capacity of three to five frames (Fig. 72), either full depth or 6⅝" depth, are excellent. Colonies in these hives will thrive under most climatic conditions that may be encountered in queen rearing, including summer heat, and they winter well in mild climates.

They are established with one comb of sealed brood and adhering bees from outlying apiaries, one comb of honey, and one empty comb. Obtaining brood and bees for these nuclei is facilitated if four or five days before the nuclei are to be established an excluder is put between the brood bodies of regular two-story full depth or 6⅝" colonies. When the nuclei are established the brood and bees are taken from the brood body that has no eggs. They should be placed on location in the mating apiary late in the afternoon, fed sugar syrup, and a ripe queen cell pressed by the base into the comb of brood. Reduction of the entrance with a robber screen will protect the new nucleus.

When these are overwintered with fall reared queens a portion may be sold as early spring comb nuclei. The queens of the remaining nuclei

Fig. 72. Standard frame five-frame nuclei.

are excellent for early packages, and the nuclei can be divided to restock the nucleus boxes from which comb nuclei were sold, or to establish new ones.

These nuclei should be fed sugar syrup in a division board feeder when the laying queens are removed. Drivert® may be poured on the bottom board, instead of feeding sugar syrup, if the area is humid or if water is readily accessible to water carriers.

When the laying queens are removed, nuclei which were queenless or are weak are reconditioned by exchanging combs for combs of brood and adhering bees from stronger nuclei. "Dead outs" are picked up and taken to the warehouse for remaking.

If nuclei are not overwintered, or are not used for queen mating during the summer months, the operation of standard frame nuclei may be uneconomical because they require considerably more bees than smaller nuclei. Bees and brood are often taken from colonies that are building up to supply package bees. For this reason most package bee shippers prefer to use smaller mating hives. Nevertheless, the beekeeper who operates a few hundred colonies or less may find the standard frame nuclei well suited to his needs. When no longer needed these nuclei can be combined into full colonies, or used to strengthen weak colonies before a honey flow, and when several are maintained in each outyard they are a ready source of replacement queens.

Divided Standard Hive Body Nuclei

The most popular divided standard hive body nuclei are standard full depth or shallow bodies divided lengthwise into two (Fig. 73), three, or

Fig. 73. Standard hive body divided into two five-frame nuclei. Entrances are at opposite ends of the body.

four compartments. Others divided crosswise into two or four compartments (Fig. 74), or both lengthwise and crosswise into four compartments (Fig. 75) are also used extensively. Entrances of the individual compartments should be located on different sides of the body, and the divisions must be bee-tight. Each compartment has its own cover of canvas or other cloth-like material, plastic sheeting, or thin board. A regular lid covers all of the compartments. The compartments may each be provided with a division board feeder, or dry sugar or Drivert® may be poured onto the bottom board if bees have ready access to water.

The nuclei with standard size frames may be established the same way as divides for colony increase. The nuclei with smaller frames may be also, if the small combs have been set in modified standard hive bodies (Fig. 76) and have been made part of the broodnest of colonies that furnish brood and bees for the nuclei. If the dividing boards of the nuclei are removed in the fall and one queen is left in the colony, the nucleus bodies themselves can become the hives for colonies that will furnish bees and brood for nuclei in the spring.

Fig. 74. Shallow body divided crosswise into four nuclei by solid division boards. Rabbets are along the sides, and entrances are on different sides.

If combs with brood are not available, the small frame nuclei are established with bulk bees that have been obtained from regular colonies. These bees are shaken into a special "bulk bee" box (Figs. 77 and 78), screened on the bottom with 8-mesh hardware cloth and with 2-inch cleats along the bottom edges of opposite sides to allow for ventilation. The top is also screened, but the ends and sides are not. Ledges are provided to support two combs with some honey. Bees cluster on the wooden sides and the combs but not on the screened bottom and top and ventilation is not obstructed. The bees remain in a cool dark place for several hours in the box before use, and are mist sprayed lightly with 30:70 or 40:60 sugar syrup several times.

The mating hives to be established, each of which must have at least one screened ventilation opening, are set in a line on the floor of a building, the entrances are closed, the feeders filled with syrup, and two combs from each set aside. The base of a ripe queen cell is pressed carefully into one of the combs remaining in the nucleus and enough bees are dipped from the bulk bee box and deposited in the nucleus to cover both sides of two of the frames. The volume of the bees required will vary with the size of the mating hive compartment. The frames that had been

Fig. 75. Hive body divided both crosswise and lengthwise into four compartments. Entrances are on different sides.

Fig. 76. Overwintered parent colony from which nuclei are established with brood and bees.

set aside are replaced in the mating hive, letting them settle on the bees by their own weight, and the hive is covered.

The filled nuclei are kept in a cool darkened place for three days and are then set out toward dusk in a mating apiary and the entrances opened.

Fig. 77. Bulk bee box screened top and bottom.

If robbing is known to be a problem, robbing screens should be placed on each nucleus (Figs. 73 and 79). While the bees are confined they process and store the syrup and renovate the combs, and the virgin emerges from her cell, so the nucleus that is set out on location is a functional unit.

Baby Nuclei

By far the most popular mating hive is the baby nucleus (Figs. 80, 81, and 82), because it requires relatively few bees to establish and little food. The individual or double boxes are easy to handle, and the laying queen can be caught quickly from them. For most/ commercial queen breeders they are the most economical of all nuclei.

They are, however, very difficult to maintain in hot weather, and in many areas should not be relied upon if queens are to be reared later than the spring months. The problem of heat can be avoided to some extent if a 1" to 2" vent hole is made in the cover and a shade board is fastened about 1" above it. Placing baby nuclei in shade during the summer months is also helpful.

Baby nuclei are established in the same way as described for broodless small frame nuclei. In the mating yard queenless or weak nuclei may be renovated by the addition of brood and bees from strong nuclei. Deadouts are taken up for reestablishment.

Fig. 78. Interior of bulk bee box showing ledges for suspension of two combs.

At the close of the queen rearing season the combs of these baby nuclei may be placed in special super bodies (Fig. 83) and stacked on colonies for emergence of the brood, after which they are stored in comb

Fig. 79. Steve Taber robber screen that is used on nuclei with round entrance holes in the body.

Fig. 80. "Baby" nucleus with three frames and feeder. The interior of the feeder has crumpled bird wire for the bees to cling to and minimize drowning.

Fig. 81. Double baby nucleus. Each side has three frames, or two frames and a thin feeder.

Fig. 82. Small nucleus larger than the usual baby nucleus.

Fig. 83. Baby nucleus combs on overwintered colony as a source of honey, brood, and bees for establishment of nuclei in the spring.

rooms and fumigated, or the stacks may be left with a queen and over-wintered as a source of brood and bees in the spring. If placed on weaker colonies, the emerged bees strengthen the colonies economically.

Mating Yard Layout and Records

The environment of the mating yard influences the mating success of the virgins. Some queen breeders state they obtain mated and laying queens from 90 to 95% of the cells that were put into nuclei. Others admit to as low as 30%. Cold, rainy, or windy weather may be associated with delayed mating and low percentages of laying queens. Lack of land-marks, and nuclei in hot sun, may also contribute to low yields of laying queens.

Nuclei should be set out in shade or semi-shade singly or in small groups, not in long rows unless landmarks are plentiful (Figs. 84 and 85). They should be protected from ants and other enemies, and not exposed directly to frequent strong winds. A suitable supply of water should be within easy flight range.

Fig. 84. Nuclei well located in partial shade in a mating yard adequately supplied with landmarks and protected from wind.

Fig. 85. Nuclei set out in small groups in the spring in a mating yard with landmarks and protected from wind.

Commercial queen breeders establish nuclei systematically so that the required number of queens are available for their packages or for individual shipment when they are needed. Establishing nuclei in successive lots so each lot will furnish queens for one day's needs, and locating the individual lots as groups in mating yards, or making one lot an entire mating yard is efficient and simplifies record keeping. The distribution of cells that will emerge on any particular day is noted on the grafting record so the location of queens ready for shipment is known.

One additional record is useful. When a cell is placed in a nucleus that date is written on the top with crayon. About fourteen days later when laying queens are removed a line is drawn through the date. If the nucleus is queenless the date is encircled, and if there is a queen in the nucleus but she is not laying the date is left unaltered. This type of record requires very little time and effort and often is valuable. If a nucleus has "missed" twice it is remade, because by that time the bees are old and will seldom produce a laying queen. The dates help to identify the mothers of the virgins. This is important in stock selection, and if susceptibility to diseases or undesirable traits appear in the progeny of any of the queens that mated from the nuclei, identifying the mother may assist the beekeeper in eliminating undesirable stock from his apiaries.

Beekeepers sometimes devise elaborate record systems for nuclei. These really serve no useful purpose, because the queen will mate when she is about 7 days old and usually will lay 3 or 4 days later. If the beekeeper harvests his queens fourteen days after the ripe cells are put in the nuclei practically all of the surviving queens will be laying, unless adverse weather has prevented mating flights.

Stones, sticks, and dirt clods can be used to briefly mark a nucleus that needs attention, and by their placement on the nucleus hives can indicate what is needed. But when the beekeeper leaves the mating yard there should be no such markers. Whatever needs to be done should be done on that visit.

Severe Robbing

Occasionally, robbing becomes a serious problem. The proper use of robber screens on the entrances of hives and nuclei will do much to prevent robbing. Should it be necessary to make prolonged examinations of full size colonies, or work with nuclei when conditions are such that robbing is sure to be a problem, the colonies can be examined peacefully within a screened cage about 3' wide, 4' deep, and 5½' to 6' tall and open at the top (Fig. 86). The weight of the cage can be minimized by constructing the frame from aluminum tubing, and horizontal bars sit-

Fig. 86. A "robber cage" is useful when lengthy examination of a colony is necessary during periods of nectar dearth.

uated along each side make convenient rods for moving the cage from colony to colony.

The robber bees pay no attention to the open top of the cage and try to reach the open hive through the sides of the cage. When the cage is moved exposing the hive to the robbers, the robber screen on the hive entrance allows the bees to protect the hive while ventilation is maintained, and robbing attempts soon subside.

Mating Queens by Instrumental Insemination

For more than a century beekeepers and bee scientists sought a way to control the matings of their breeding queens, especially those of the queen mothers. More recently beekeepers who produce queens on a large commercial scale have become interested in the possibility of using instrumental insemination to mate the queens they sell that are to become mothers of field, or producing, colonies. This is possible, and, in fact, is being done. Instrumental insemination is practical, fast, and economically competitive with "open" mating of queens from nuclei. This is not to say, however, that every beekeeper, nor every queen breeder, should abandon open matings and depend upon instrumental insemination for mating all of his queens.

Instrumental insemination does have some distinct advantages over open mating of queens. Not only can the mating of the queen mothers be controlled so that evaluation and selection of breeding stock can be more meaningful, but specific matings can be made among breeders, that is, selected virgins from certain queen mothers can be mated to selected drones from certain drone mothers to give the best hereditary background, with the stock available, to the queens and their progeny that will compose the colonies to be used in the field. Virgin queens can be instrumentally inseminated day or night, in good weather or bad, and each will have a normal or near normal number of spermatozoa in the spermatheca; enough to influence the performances of the queens and outlast the usual productive life of queens in field colonies.

There are additional advantages; and there are also disadvantages. One of the most serious of these is the necessity to have a continuing and abundant supply of healthy, mature drones of the proper stock readily available during the entire time the queens are being inseminated. This one requirement alone can bring dismay to the beekeeper until he accepts the fact he must rear and mature his drones with the same care and systematic planning he observes in rearing his virgins.

A second problem inherent in instrumental insemination involves selection and training of inseminators. Instrumental insemination as it is done today is not especially difficult to learn or perform. Nevertheless, it is precise work, and many people do not have the disposition to cope with the demands of such work, and even fewer can maintain efficiency hour after hour for a season. Thus, when great numbers of queens are inseminated in a few weeks it is essential that an adequate pool of skilled inseminators be established.

Sanitation is of paramount importance. Queens become easily infected with organisms during the insemination process that cause the death of the queen if strict sanitation is not observed. Instruments should be carefully and frequently sterilized, hands must be washed frequently with soap and water, and the inseminator must be alert to the possibility that the semen has become contaminated with drone or queen fecal matter. A routine of sanitary precautions is essential for each inseminator to follow.

The cost of the instruments and other equipment necessary for a successful insemination program can be considerable. While with proper care the instruments will last indefinitely, the investment in them is not justified unless they will be used to near their capacity.

Special beekeeping methods and equipment, and careful planning and scheduling of various operations are unavoidable.

Introduction of instrumentally inseminated queens must be made with care unless the queens have laid or eggs are developing in the ovaries. Attempts, sometimes made by the bees, to immediately supersede instrumentally inseminated queens that have not laid before introduction may require examination of colonies with such queens to be made within two weeks after the queen is placed in the colony. However, once the brood-nest is established the tendency to supersede disappears. The tendency of immediate supersedure occurs also when queens from nuclei are introduced. It is not limited to instrumentally inseminated queens.

It should be recognized that though instrumental insemination of virgin queens is a practical and successful specialized beekeeping activity, it seems unlikely that instrumental insemination will become part of the routine of most beekeepers, but will, instead, be used by a relatively few beekeepers who will mate breeding queens for other beekeepers, sell queens for breeding stock, and produce queens for the package bees of other bee shippers. Nevertheless, instrumental insemination is a part of beekeeping that all commerical beekeepers should know something about, because it is inevitable that their operations will be affected in some way by bee stock that has been developed or produced with the aid of instrumental insemination.

Anyone who desires to actually instrumentally inseminate queen bees should first of all become acquainted with books and papers dealing with the subject, such as those by Laidlaw (1977), Mackensen and Tucker (1970), and Ruttner (1976). Then, if at all possible, two or three days should be spent under the tutelage of someone skilled in the operation. Only then should an investment be made in instruments and equipment. By all means start on a modest scale. Become adept in all aspects of instrumental insemination before entertaining thoughts of expansion.

Planning the Insemination

When enough skill in the technique of instrumental insemination has been acquired to assure success, the work should be planned so the virgins and their potential mates will exist and be the best age for insemination. This is not difficult when few queens are to be inseminated, but when large numbers of queens are to be inseminated an easily followed scheduling system should be used. The scheduling form devised by Laidlaw (1954), (Fig. 87), has been used for many years in the program at the

MATINGS

STOCKS and MATINGS							DRONES						VIRGINS					INSEM
Virgin's Mother		Virgin	Drone's Mother				Comb in Breeder	Comb in Feeder	Cage Drone Brood	Drone Emerg. Date	Cage Drones	Drones Mature	Comb in Breeder	Comb in Feeder	Graft	Cells out and Excl.	Clip or Mark	
Colony No.	Queen No.	Mating	Mating	Mating	Queen No.	Colony No.												

Fig. 87. Scheduling form for use in production of instrumentally inseminated queens.

University of California, Davis (UCD) and might be useful as a model that can be modified for devising a scheduling procedure suitable for a beekeeper's particular method of operation.

Securing Mature Drones From Selected Drone Mothers

In case only a few queens are to be inseminated, the selected drone mother colonies will probably have enough mature drones for the inseminations. The drone mother colonies may be isolated from each other and from other bees to minimize drifting of drones, and they should be fed throughout the time drones are being reared and matured unless there are at least moderate flows of nectar and pollen. The drones to be used may be picked off of the outer combs, with care being taken to select the most active drones, which will be further characterized by a large thorax and a small abdomen. The actual size of the drone is judged by the size of the thorax which does not change after emergence. In contrast, the abdomen of a newly emerged drone is large because the testes, which lie in the expandable abdomen, are still filled with spermatozoa. As the spermatozoa move to the seminal vesicles the testes shrink and finally become mere bits of amorphous tissue. This is accompanied by the abdomen's becoming much reduced in size.

The drones from these colonies may also be caught at the entrance before or after their flight when inseminations are made in the afternoon. In any case, only some of the drones will yield semen. Those that yield only a small amount should not be used, because their use over several generations may incorporate male sterility in the stock, as occurred several times at UCD, supposedly from this cause, (Laidlaw, unpublished).

Drones from drone mother colonies may be emerged and matured above an excluder, and the drones trapped and caged in the afternoon as they try to fly, or picked from the combs and caged early in the morning before drone flight, or late in the afternoon after flight has ceased. Such caged drones must be fed with candy or sugar syrup or by bees in a hive because they soon starve otherwise. Drones that have not flown or had a recent flight may have an accumulation of feces that can contribute to infection of queens that are inseminated with them unless care is taken to prevent the feces from contaminating the semen and the instruments.

These methods of securing mates for queens are not suitable when large numbers of queens are to be instrumentally inseminated. The beekeeper who instrumentally inseminates thousands of queens for sale must also rear and mature drones by the tens of thousands.

Drone combs are put into drone mother colonies, one to each colony, about 40 days before the drones will be needed. Approximately five days later a new drone comb is given to each drone mother, and the previous drone combs, which should have eggs and some larvae, are transferred to the second body, above an excluder, of strong queenright or queenless colonies for feeding and development. Three or four drone combs may be put into each feeding colony and the remainder of the body filled with brood and pollen combs. The feeding colonies are fed syrup and pollen patties constantly. At the time of transfer, the drone emergence date is determined for each comb of drone eggs and larvae and is recorded on the schedule sheet.

The drones may be permitted to emerge in the feeding colonies. If this is done they should be marked so their stock or line or their particular drone mother can be identified. Cale used paint from a spray can for marking drones. The opening of the can is enlarged slightly so the paint will splatter rather than be a fine spray. By quick movements of the can, held about 18 inches from the comb, those drones on a comb can be marked almost instantaneously. An entrance is provided so the drones can fly, or the frames of marked drones are put into a specially made-up queenless colony to mature. Flying drones have very little accumulated feces and their use is cleaner than the use of drones that have been caged for some time.

Fig. 88. Comb cage for emerging drones in an incubator. The sides which may be either screen or excluder fit into top and bottom channels so they can be slipped sideways to expose the drones on the comb.

Laidlaw (1954) cages the drone brood the day before emergence in a comb cage (Fig. 88). The drones are emerged in an incubator and are

Fig. 89. Cage for maturing drones in a nursery colony.

picked from the comb and caged on the day of their emergence in drone maturing cages (Fig. 89) that accommodate 50 to 60 drones, four of which fit into a frame. The drones are matured in nursery colonies and are ready for use when they are at least ten days old. These drones will have considerable feces, and care must be taken to prevent contamination of the semen when the semen is collected in the syringe.

When great numbers of mature drones are needed and it is not necessary to identify drones from a particular mother, the time required to cage the newly emerged drones can be greatly shortened by emerging several combs of drone brood in a hive body that is provided with detachable screens on top and bottom. This is placed in an incubator. In the morning of each day of emergence the body is set on a shaker box, from which the excluder in the funnel has been removed, and the drones are jarred from the combs into the bottom part of the shaker box. They are then dipped up with a scoop that measures approximately the correct number of drones for a maturing cage and are dumped into the maturing cages.

It is emphasized that drones matured in cages usually have more feces than those that have free flight. This is a disadvantage. Also, sometimes half or more of the drones may die in maturing cages before they are old enough to use. On the other hand, most of the surviving drones matured in cages yield semen in abundance. Their source is easily identifiable, and they are obtainable quickly at any time. Whether the occasional premature death of a large proportion of the drones is unusual is unknown. It is quite possible the same proportion of drones from the same drone mother would have died had the drones had free flight, but the loss of drones would be less noticeable because of the absence of dead drones.

Pre-insemination Care of Virgin Queens

Virgin queens may be emerged in nuclei and returned to the nuclei following insemination, or emerged in nursery cages in nursery colonies and either returned in cages to the nursery temporarily or introduced to nuclei. The emergence of queens in nuclei and their return to nuclei following insemination is probably best when a few hundred queens or less are instrumentally inseminated. Any style nucleus is suitable, but if the queens are to remain in the nuclei for several weeks or months the larger nuclei are preferable.

The nuclei are established or re-celled in the same way as are those for open mated queens. When the nuclei are set on location, or re-celled, the entrances are excludered, and within a day or two after emergence the virgins are clipped. They may be marked at this time, also. If preferred, the virgin may be emerged in a nursery cage that is put in the nucleus when it is made up or re-celled.

When the queen is five or six days old, she is given a five to ten minute exposure to carbon dioxide and is returned to her nucleus. When she is seven to ten days old, she is inseminated and is returned to her nucleus by dropping her, while she is still anaesthetized, between the frames, or, if she has revived, she can be permitted to run from her cage onto the frames of the nucleus. Three to five days later she should be laying, and the excluder may be removed from the entrance.

The preliminary exposure of the queen to carbon dioxide may be omitted and a similar but post-insemination carbon dioxide treatment administered instead. There is no particular post-insemination care the beekeeper must give queens returned to their nuclei, because the bees attend the queen and accord her the treatment she would have received had she flown to mate.

A more labor efficient management must be devised when several thousand queens are instrumentally inseminated in a short time. It is better, then, to emerge queens in nursery cages in nursery colonies where the bees care for the virgins. Carbon dioxide can be administered to many caged virgins at the same time. Further advantages are that virgin queens which do not quite meet the standard of the beekeeper are easier for him to discard from nursery cages than are those already introduced into nuclei, and the virgins are readily available at any time in quantities that are surplus to the number to be inseminated. But queens inseminated from nursery cages must be introduced to nuclei or full colonies and this involves post-insemination care.

Post-insemination Care of Instrumentally Inseminated Queens

As is well known, the introduction of virgins that are more than a few hours old to either full colonies or nuclei is much more difficult than the introduction of laying queens under the same environmental conditions. One might infer from this that the pheromones of virgins and laying queens, or queens that have laid, differ in some way. Assuming this is so, the post-insemination care of queens that were inseminated from nursery colonies should at least induce the formation of eggs in the ovaries, and preferably bring about oviposition. The migration of the sperm from the oviducts to the spermatheca is influenced by the temperature surrounding the queen for the first few hours following injection of the semen into the oviducts, and possibly by the activity of the queen herself. These factors should also be considered in post-insemination queen care.

All of the conditions that contribute to proper post-insemination care of instrumentally inseminated queens are present in colonies where the queen is loose among the bees, except the little understood cause of the prompt initiation of egg development which appears to be present in some cases and not in others. About two-thirds of the instrumentally inseminated queens that are free among the bees may lay promptly following insemination and without further exposure to carbon dioxide, that is, with only the one exposure the queen receives during insemination.

Mackensen found that two 10-minute treatments, spaced a day apart, with carbon dioxide caused nearly all queens so treated to lay fairly promptly whether inseminated or not. Now, instrumentally inseminated queens routinely receive one carbon dioxide treatment during the process of insemination and another exposure before or after insemination.

Queens that are inseminated from nursery colonies should be returned to nursery colonies that are arranged so that young larvae are next to the screens of the nursery cages; and the queens should be kept in properly maintained nurseries after insemination for one to two weeks. Nursery colonies should be fed sugar syrup and pollen cakes continuously so the nurse bees that feed the young larvae may secrete an excess of royal jelly and probably share it with the inseminated queens. In many cases, inseminated queens in nurseries will drop eggs in the cages; and the initiation of egg development in the ovarioles is likely to have taken place in queens that had not dropped eggs.

Fig. 90. Cage for post-insemination care of queens that were emerged in nursery colonies.

Beekeepers are reluctant to buy young queens that have not laid, regardless of how well they are inseminated. Thus, the final step in the production of instrumentally inseminated queens on a commercial scale is to devise methods to bring about oviposition without resorting to use of the usual nuclei. Laidlaw (1973, unpublished) designed and used a special cage (Fig. 90), four of which would fit in a frame. Following insemination, the inseminated queens were confined to the cages and put into a nursery colony. Two to four days later bees were permitted to enter the cages through excluders. Some of the queens laid before bees entered the cage, and others soon afterward. In some cases when bees were allowed to enter the cages too rapidly the queens were killed. The nursery colony was fed sugar syrup and pollen cake constantly, and sometimes pollen was put into some of the comb cells near the top of the cage for the bees to eat after they gained access to the cage. The queens confined alone were provided a small amount of candy made with invert sugar syrup, pollen, and powdered sugar, or with candy made with powdered sugar and a mixture of invert sugar syrup and royal jelly.

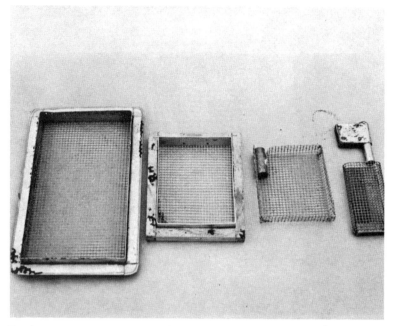

Fig. 91.   a   b   c   d
Introducing cages: (a) and (b) push-in cages; (c) Cale push-in cage with provision for bees to release the queen; (d) Miller type cage also with provision for
bees to release the queen.

Foti, also in 1973, placed newly inseminated queens in cages of his
design that had comb, a screen side, and an entrance over which was fastened a piece of excluder. The cage was stocked with bees, an instrumentally inseminated queen was put in among them, and several of the cages
were set on top of frames of a colony and enclosed by a hive body. The
bees "foraged" from the cages, returning to their own cages, and the
queens laid in the comb.

It should be noted that in these two methods a small colony was
established in each cage, much like a nucleus.

Introduction of Instrumentally Inseminated Queens

Instrumentally inseminated queens that have laid are no more difficult to introduce to colonies than are open mated queens that have
laid. Instrumentally inseminated queens that have not laid, like open
mated queens that have not laid, require more care in their introduction.

The safest practical method of introduction is by the use of a push-in cage (Fig. 91). Another method that is quite successful is simply to keep the queen confined in a shipping or nursery cage, in the colony to be requeened, for five to seven days after which she is released among the bees if the bees are quiet and show no animosity toward her while she is in the cage. Constant feeding of the colony enhances success by this method, or by any other. The cage in which the queen is confined may be filled to crowding with bees swollen with honey from the colony receiving the queen; bees filled with honey will not harm a queen, and by the time the honey in the honey sacs is nearly depleted the queen is accepted by the bees in the cage.

Insemination of Potential Breeding Queens For Other Beekeepers

It seems to be unlikely that many beekeepers will establish laboratories for instrumental insemination, but most of the queen breeders, and many honey producers who rear their own queens, should utilize the services of the laboratories that exist to have potential breeding queens mated, a practice already widely used in Europe, and a service that was provided by the University of California, Davis for many years to California queen breeders. If such a laboratory, perhaps better termed an insemination center, is reasonably close a beekeeper can bring nuclei with five to ten-day old virgin queens, confined to the nuclei by excluders, to the laboratory and leave them for the queens to be inseminated and checked afterward. Should the distance be great between the beekeeper and the laboratory, virgins and drones can be shipped by mail or other carrier. A good shipping cage for this purpose is shown in Fig. 92. The queen is confined with attendants to two holes at one end of the cage and a third hole is filled with queen cage candy. The remainder of the cage is provided with candy in two or three holes and has thirty to forty mature drones and a like number of worker attendants. A second and similar cage accompanies this cage which has three holes of the larger compartment filled with queen cage candy and is stocked with about 100 workers, preferably young bees and preferably from the colony that will receive the inseminated queen. Upon arrival at the insemination center, the queen is exposed to carbon dioxide for a period of five to ten minutes. The next day she is inseminated with semen from the drones that were sent with her, and, while still anaesthetized, is dropped among the bees in the second cage, that have also been lightly anaesthetized or which have been fed to repletion with sugar syrup. The cages with inseminated queens are kept overnight in an incubator or strong colony, and are then returned to the beekeeper. The introduction of these queens must be done carefully, pref-

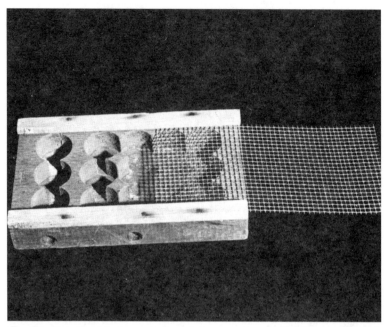

Fig. 92. Cage for shipping a virgin and drones to be mated to her to an insemination center.

erably with a push-in cage. Ten days after the queens begin to lay, the colonies are examined and any queen cells found on the combs are destroyed.

CHAPTER V

Use of Queens

Young queens mated from nuclei are ready for use as soon as they begin to lay. They are now as good as they will ever be, but they can be injured or killed by careless or inept handling during or after their removal from their mating nuclei. The hobby beekeeper and the commercial queen breeder must both observe care in the treatment of queens and employ methods of handling that will not diminish their value as colony mothers. These precautions are not difficult to adhere to if one knows how queens should be cared for and what things can be detrimental.

Caging Queens

Nuclei are sometimes elevated on posts or stands, but most are simply set out on the ground. A "hive seat," or queen yard stool (Fig. 93), can make catching queens and re-celling the nuclei easier for the beekeeper in such circumstances. It not only contributes to the comfort of the bee-

Fig. 93. A light stool is a welcome aid for examining nuclei that rest on the ground.

Fig. 94. A queen may be caged by "herding" her into the entry hole.

keeper, but assists him in transporting empty queen cages, and also caged queens until they are put into carrying boxes for transport to the warehouse.

Queens should be handled with care at all times and especially when they are being caged. They may be "herded" into queen cages by placing the open end of the cage against the comb and with the fingers of the other hand guiding the queen into the cage (Fig. 94). Most frequently, however, the queen is picked up from behind by wings on both sides. Her head is put into the entrance hole, and, as her front legs grasp the cage, her wings are released and with fingers behind her (Fig. 95), she is gently prevented from backing up. The queen should never be held by one wing or one leg because she may twist and injure herself.

When queens are shipped individually there must be attendants in the cages, which should be young bees, preferably enlarged with honey in the honey stomach. These are picked from the comb by both pairs of wings, and the head and thorax are pushed into the cage entry hole (Fig. 96). The hole is then closed between attendants with the forefinger or thumb

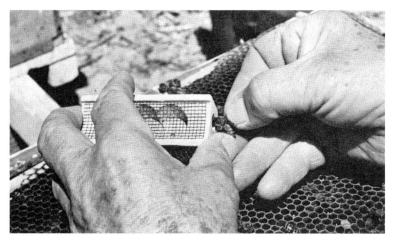

Fig. 95. Queens are most often caged by grasping the queen by both pairs of wings, then inserting her head into the entry hole of the cage, and letting her walk into the cage.

Fig. 96. Worker attendant bees are caged in a manner similar to caging the queen.

Fig. 97.   a   b   c
Cages for shipping queens: (a) two-hole cage that is used for shipping queens
with package bees (The queen is caged without attendants or candy); (b) a metal
strip is tacked to the back of the two-hole cage for suspending the cage in a package of bees; (c) three-hole cage for shipping queens with attendants and queen
cage candy.

to prevent escape of the bees. Finally the end closure cork or perforated
metal is pushed in. Seven to ten attendants should be put into each cage.
Some queen breeders load the cages by means of various devices with
gorged workers before the queens are caught. When many queens are
shipped individually much time can be saved by caging attendants first in
this way.

Queens Caged For Package Bees

Queens shipped with package bees are caged from their nuclei in
2-hole cages without candy or attendants. The cage has a strip of metal
attached to the back near one end for fastening the cage in the package
so it will hang among the bees near the feeder can (Fig. 97b). The filled
cages are fastened into special frames (Fig. 98), and are taken in venti-
lated carrying boxes, that have a frame with honey and enough bees to
care for the queens, from the mating yards to the warehouse and from
the warehouse to the apiaries where packages are being filled.

If the queens are to remain caged for a day or a week or more before shipment, the frames of caged queens are transferred to "bank colonies" which are strong, queenless, broodless, and free flying colonies, usually one-story, with spaces between empty combs for the frames of caged

Fig. 98. Two-hole cages with queens in a special frame for transport or for temporary storage in a bank colony.

queens. These colonies are fed 40:60 sugar syrup with fumagillin constantly and each week receive one to 1½ pounds of young bees.

Queens Caged For Individual Shipment

Queens that are to be shipped individually are put into 3-hole cages (Fig. 97c), one chamber of which is provisioned with queen cage candy. As the queens are caged, they are placed in a container, such as a hive seat and then a box, to protect them from sun or from cold until they are taken to the place they will be prepared for shipment.

Queen Cage Candy

Queen cage candy is made of powdered sugar, or Drivert®, and invert sugar syrup. Invert sugar syrup can be made by the beekeeper but purchase of the syrup is more convenient. One type of commercial invert sugar syrup that is used extensively by queen breeders is Nulomoline.® Unfortunately, candy made with this syrup soon hardens. The firmness to which the candy is made with Nulomoline® should vary somewhat with the temperature to which the queens will be exposed in shipping. Too soft

Fig. 99. One way to hold a queen for clipping.

candy will run in the cage killing the bees, and the bees may starve if the candy is too hard. Queen cage candy made with honey is best for shipping queens because it can be made quite firm and it does not harden quickly. It remains cohesive, pliable, and moist for long periods even when constantly exposed to the air, but because it might be contaminated with spores of American foulbrood from the honey, its use in shipping queens is prohibited. Isomerized high fructose corn syrup has many of the properties of honey and seems to be suitable for bee food. When used as a syrup for making queen cage candy, the candy resembles that made with honey and there is no danger of transmission of bee diseases through the candy. Type 50 sugar syrup, which is 77% solids of which 50% is invert sugar, may also be used.

In making queen cage candy, the syrup is poured into a bowl, glycerine is mixed with Nulomoline® at the rate of three tablespoons to 1½ gallons, and powdered sugar or Drivert® is added with stirring until the mixture becomes thick or dough-like. It is then set in the sun, tightly covered, for a day so that the syrup and sugar become thoroughly mixed. Before use, a portion is put on a board sprinkled with powdered sugar and is kneaded with frequent addition of small amounts of powdered sugar until the candy becomes firm, and a ball of the candy will flatten very little on standing. When a small amount is pinched from the ball the consistency should be cohesive, slightly sticky, but not stick to the·fingers. If it crumbles, the candy is too dry, and if it is quite soft and sticks to the fingers, it needs to have more sugar worked into it.

The cages of queens shipped in warm weather should be provisioned with firm candy, otherwise the candy will run. Candy for shipment in cool or cold weather may be made to feel a little soft, but a ball should not flatten much on standing, nor should the candy, though it may feel sticky, stick to the fingers.

One hole, which should be waxed, of the 3-hole shipping cage is filled with candy, and a square of wax paper or plastic film is laid over the top before the wire is attached to the cage. The hole in the end of the cage that leads to the candy may be closed with cork or a cardboard disc or covered with a strip of cardboard. The Pinard cage used extensively in California may have a bee entry hole at the opposite end of the cage closed with cork, because when the cages are stacked the raised edges provide for ventilation between the cages (Fig. 97c). Other queen shipping cages do not have the raised edges, and, unless they have ventilation saw kerfs along the sides, cross strips are inserted between stacked cages. The entry hole of each may be closed with a disc of special perforated metal.

Clipping and Marking

Sometimes the queens are to be clipped or marked before they are caged. Probably the safest way to hold the queen for clipping is by the thorax between the thumb and forefinger of one hand while half of the wings on one side of the queen are cut with small scissors held in the other hand (Fig. 99). If the right wings are clipped in even years and the left wings in odd years, the beekeeper is better able to judge the age of his queens in his colonies.

After a queen is clipped, she may be marked by a bit of paint on the dorsal side of the thorax (Fig. 100). Many kinds of paint are used, but it should be quick drying and non-offensive to the attendant bees. One of the better and more easily available paints is liquid paper correction fluid that can be obtained in several colors to coincide with the International color code which is as follows:

White or grey for years ending in 1 or 6
Yellow for years ending in 2 or 7
Red for years ending in 3 or 8
Green for years ending in 4 or 9
Blue for years ending in 5 or 0

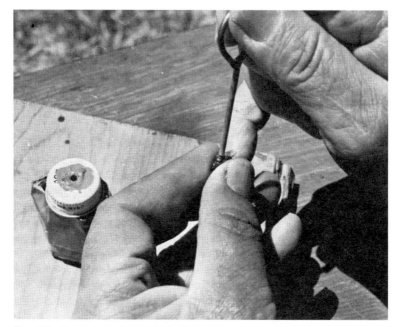

Fig. 100. Queen is marked with the flat end of marking probe of the paint bottle.

Other paints may be used, such as fingernail polish, or model airplane "dope." One of the paints used many years ago, and one of the best, is dry pigment suspended in clear, white shellac. In scientific work, paints have been largely superseded by colored, and often numbered, plastic or metal disks that are glued to the back of the thorax of the queens.

The paint is easily applied with a wire or nail that has one end flat and the other end attached to a knob. The paint bottle is closed with a stopper through which a hole, having a diameter sufficient for the daubing probe to slide through it, has been made in the center (Fig. 100). When such a probe is withdrawn, the paint on the sides is scraped off into the bottle leaving only the paint on the flat end, and when this is touched to the thorax a clean round mark is left. Care must be taken not to get paint over the spiracles of the thorax.

Re-celling

Queens are usually removed from an entire lot, block, or group of nuclei the same day. The nuclei are fed sugar syrup, Drivert,® or dry

Fig. 101. Caged queens in three-hole cages packaged for shipment.

fine granulated sugar after the queens are removed from them, and the same day or the next day a ripe queen cell is given. This is "re-celling." The introduction of virgins to nuclei was once favored, but virgin introduction is difficult and is no longer practiced by most queen breeders. For this reason virgin nursery cages and virgin nursery colonies are seldom used except in experimental work.

Shipping

Shipments of single queens can have a standard queen cage mailing cover over the screen, or several cages can be stacked under one cover. One or a few caged queens can also be mailed in manila envelopes if several holes are punched near the envelope margin.

Larger shipments of many queens should be carefully and securely bundled or crated. "V"-grooved strips can be tacked to the corners of stacked queen cages to hold the cages together, or the cages may be bound together with staples and tape. The cages can be layered in a small crate that resembles a package bee cage (Fig. 101). This crate is made of thin "shook" boards, with the sides closed with plastic screen fastened to the crate with wooden strips. The top layer of queen cages has the screen of the queen cages turned downward toward the other queen cages, and any space between this layer and the top of the shipping crate is stuffed with crumpled paper to prevent any movement of the queen cages.

If the weather is warm, or if the queens are to go a considerable distance, two or three drops of water applied to the screens of the queen cages is beneficial, but never apply more than this; the bees will take the water and if too much is applied, the bees regurgitate it and the bees and queen may be lost.

An inspection certificate must be attached to each queen shipment, and each shipment should be prominently marked as LIVE BEES.

Introduction of Queens

There is probably no more vexous problem associated with beekeeping than that of acceptance of a new queen by a colony. Many methods and special cages have been employed over the years to ensure that the new queen will be accepted by the bees. None of the methods is perfect, but some are consistently more successful than others.

As all beekeepers know, a queen is most readily accepted if a honey flow is in progress, even a light one, so that both field bees and house bees are fully occupied with their duties. If there is no flow, the colony to be requeened should be fed 40:60 syrup. It is important that the feeder does not become empty during the period of introduction because an empty feeder ends the flow.

There are other considerations to be observed in introducing queens. The colony should be queenless, and the bees should have ample time and opportunity to become "acquainted" with the new queen while she is protected in a cage in the hive. While caged, her specific pheromones become distributed throughout the colony so the bees recognize her as their queen. Pheromones of laying queens must differ in some respects from those of virgin queens so the queen should be laying, have laid, or be ready to lay with eggs developing in the ovaries, because laying queens are much less difficult to introduce than virgins. Another method of introduction is to so demoralize the bees that when the queen is placed among them she has become part of the colony by the time the colony is again organized.

Push-in Cage

One of the surest ways to introduce a queen to a colony is by a "push-in" cage. The simplest is made of 8-mesh hardware cloth and measures at least 3" by 3½" and is ⅝" deep. It may have a 1¼" long piece of 7/16" inside diameter metal tubing attached to the inner surface of one side and opening to the exterior (Fig. 91a, b, c). When used, the tube is filled with queen cage candy, and the bees eat the candy to release the queen after several days. More elaborate push-in cages may have a metal rim inside a wooden or metal flange to which hardware cloth or screen wire is attached on the upper side. The rim extends about ⅜" below the flange. The flange impedes the bees' cutting the comb beneath the rim and entering the cage too soon.

In using a push-in cage a dark comb from which bees are emerging is selected and the queen is put on the comb in an area that has both open cells and some emerging bees and, if possible, some honey. The cage is placed over the queen and is pushed into the comb to almost the comb midrib or until the cage flange rests on the comb. If provision has been made for the bees to release the queen, the cage may be removed when convenient. If the cage does not have a candy tube, the cage should be removed about five days later to release the queen and the emerged bees.

In such a cage, the queen begins to lay promptly and is accepted by the emerged bees in the cage with her. She is in the cage long enough before release for the colony also to accept her, as they usually do. To give the queen reasonable exposure to the colony, the push-in cage should measure no smaller than 3 x 3½ inches. A cage 4 x 5 inches or 5 x 6 inches is preferred by some beekeepers.

The Miller Introducing Cage

The Miller introducing cage has long been popular and is one of the more successful queen introducing devices. It is a rectangular screen cage. One end is permanently closed, the other closed with a stopper that has two tubes: a short one having excluder over the inner end, and a long one that is open at both ends (Fig. 91c). Both tubes are filled with queen cage candy when the cage is used. The queen is placed alone in the cage, and the cage is placed between two combs of sealed or emerging brood in such a way the bees can cover the screen of both sides and have access to the candy in the tubes. The candy in the short tube is soon eaten and one bee at a time enters the cage with the queen. The queen will emerge from the cage when the candy of the long tube is eaten. This cage is quite satisfactory. In practical use the size of the cage varies with the preference of the beekeeper using it, but it should be long enough and wide enough for many bees to cover the screen because in such introductions maximum exposure of the protected queen to the bees is important. Jay Smith described his excellent versions of the push-in and Miller cages in his books (1923, 1949).

Queens with or without attendant bees are often introduced in the mailing cages in which they were shipped. If the candy hole of the cage is covered with paper or cork, this is removed. To reduce the time required to release the queen, a hole may be punched through the candy with a probe, such as a match stem. The cage is placed between two combs of sealed or emerging brood so that the screen of the cage is exposed to the bees of the colony. Usually the queen will be out of the cage in two days and will be laying. This method, though widely used, is not as certain as the push-in cage, however.

Other Methods

Queens may be introduced from nuclei by placing the frames of the nucleus together with the queen and bees into the middle of the colony receiving the queen. Feeding the receiving colony for several days prior to giving them the queen enhances the success of this method if no nectar is being gathered, as does a light spraying of the colony with 40:60 sugar syrup during the transfer.

A rather laborious method that is quite successful is to shake the bees of the colony onto the ground in front of the hive. After the bees are going into the hive, drop the queen among them; she will walk in with the bees and usually will become part of the colony.

When a queen is so valuable no chance can be taken that she will be killed, she can be released onto a comb of emerging brood with no bees, which is then placed in a hive body above an 8-mesh hardware cloth screen over a strong colony. After enough bees have emerged to cover much of the comb and the queen begins to lay, the body is set off on a bottom board, and emerging brood is added at frequent intervals until the colony is strong enough to care for itself. It is advisable to use a robber screen and leave a very small entrance while the colony is weak.

Hive Records

Most beekeepers do not use queen records on the hives. Nevertheless, hive queen records can be very useful, especially if the beekeeper has an interest in improving his stock. They should be simple. The date a new queen is given to the colony, her source or stock, and how she was marked or clipped can be written in pencil in a corner of the bottom body of the hive. An appraisal of a stock soon develops if colony performances, as judged by observation, are associated with their stock. Supers of honey removed can be jotted down quickly, and later this information can be retrieved for stock comparisons.

CHAPTER VI

Package Bee Production

The production of package bees in the United States is a specialized beekeeping activity of northern California and the southern states. It is intimately associated with queen rearing because each package requires a young mated queen. The packaging and shipment of bees for establishment of colonies in northern states and Canada takes place in a relatively short period in early spring from about April 1 to May 10, after which the colonies from which the bees were taken may be used for honey production or pollination. Package bees are produced and shipped commercially by a relatively few beekeepers who make this beekeeping specialty their principal business, with honey production and pollination ancillary activities. On a commercial scale, package bee production demands coordination of queen and bee rearing, careful scheduling, and advance preparation for the intense period of shipment. On a smaller scale, package bees can readily be produced by a beekeeper for his own use.

Colony Management

Colony management for package bee production differs little from management for honey production, except, that since the product of the hive is bees instead of honey, colonies must become strong very early in the year, much earlier than is usually desirable for honey production.

The package bee producer's new year begins during the middle or latter part of the shipping period or soon after the current shipping season ends. It is then that colonies are requeened with queen cells or with queens that were reared toward the close of package bee shipping. "Divides" are made at this time to replace dead or weak colonies and each is given a queen cell. Vigorous queens are essential for early bees, and yearly requeening of the bee-producing colonies is required. After requeening and during the remainder of the year, the colonies may be utilized for honey production or pollination, and final selection of breeder queens is made. In the late summer and early fall, particular attention is given the colonies to ensure adequate and proper placement of pollen supplies and honey for winter and early spring. Unless there is sufficient incoming pollen late in the fall to encourage moderate brood rearing, a mixture of pollen and a pollen supplement is fed. The same mixture may be fed in late winter before spring pollen becomes available in quantity, and later in spring if inclement weather interferes with pollen collecting.

Pollen supplements vary in composition and use with the beekeeper using them and with availability of the various components. The search for satisfactory pollen supplements and substitutes has accelerated in recent years but as yet without complete success. It is reasonable to assume that as more knowledge of the nutritional requirements of the bee colony is gained, pollen supplements, or even substitutes, will be developed that will approach the brood rearing value of the most nutritional pollens.

The pollen supplements that are currently in use are readily taken by the bees, and feeding them at proper times results in early and heavy brood rearing. One of the components is always pollen, about 5 to 25% of the dry mixture, which seems to be necessary to entice the bees to eat the supplement. The non-pollen protein part of the supplement may be any of a number of substances or mixtures among which are expeller-processed soybean flour, Torula dried yeast Type S, Torutein-10,® and brewers yeast. One formula used extensively consists of a mixture of one-half Torula yeast or Torutein-10® and one-half brewers yeast, plus pollen and Type 50 syrup. One-hundred pounds of the Torula-brewers yeast dry mix is thoroughly mixed with 120 pounds of Type 50 syrup to which 5 pounds of pollen suspended in water was added.

The pollen is thawed if it is frozen, and is then suspended in water and mixed with the syrup. The dry mixture is added to the syrup and pollen until the supplement stands like dough, when it is poured or pressed into molds. It may be left in these to "ripen" for 24 to 48 hours before it is sliced into approximately one-pound cakes.

The mixture of pollen and other substances is sometimes fed dry in the hive or in the open, and may have Drivert,® powdered sugar or finely granulated sugar as a component. Dry supplements are usually significantly wasted by being ejected from the hive entrance by the bees.

Sugar syrup, 1 part sugar and 1 part water, is fed in the fall if needed for winter stores, and a lighter syrup, 4 parts sugar and 6 parts water, may be fed in spring to encourage brood rearing.

It is essential in package bee production that the colonies be strong early in the year, earlier than is usually desirable for honey production if the main honey flow occurs in late spring or early summer. Colonies that are strong very early in the season may have a greater tendency to swarm than those reaching a population peak shortly before a main honey flow. Reducing the population by using some early bees from the colonies for establishment of cell builders and nuclei and by shipping excess bees later in packages controls swarming. Nevertheless, during protracted periods of inclement weather, when queen mating and package bee shipments are delayed, the loss of bees through swarming can be serious.

Good management and skillful beekeeping are thus essential to timely and maximum production of bees for packages. All of the elements of good beekeeping are involved, such as vigorous queens, abundant food, ventilation for moisture elimination, colony protection from winds and water, placement so hives are exposed to the sun, swarm control, and control of diseases and enemies.

Package Bee Supplies

The package bee shipper utilizes the winter months to prepare equipment and supplies for the shipping season. Package cages are made, and queen cages made or bought. California shippers buy precut package cages and assemble them in the winter. They also buy Pinard type queen cages, two-hole for shipping queens without attendants in packages (Fig. 97), and three-hole for shipping queens individually with attendants (Fig. 101). Southern shippers usually make the cages for the bees from stock lumber, and also make the queen cages themselves. This activity helps to provide employment for permanent personnel.

The size of the package cages may vary, but have become standardized in California. Standardization is necessary for shipping by truck because the truck bodies are built specifically for the transport of package bees. The cage for the popular two-pound package measures 8⅝" high x 12" long x 6" wide (Fig. 102), and for the three-pound package 8⅝" tall x 16" long x 6" wide. A four-pound package with two cages of queens is preferred by some beekeepers who split the package of bees upon receipt to establish two colonies. Four pounds of bees are shipped in cages 10⅛" high x 16" long x 6" wide. The sides of the cages are screened. The top, bottom, and ends are solid. Each package is provided with a number 2½ feeder can that is inserted into a hole in the top of the cage and rests on a cross bar supported at each end by a perpendicular bar nailed to the top and bottom of the cage to form an "H"-shaped support, or on a "U"-shaped support nailed across the middle of the cage to the cage bottom (Fig. 102).

The type of can opening used varies among shippers. With few exceptions, the cans have either small holes in the lid to give the bees access to the feed or a large central hole covered with Indian Head Spring Made Decorator line or similar cotton cloth. The cloth patch may be fastened to the inside of the lid with automobile body repair speed spot putty that has been thinned with auto speed putty thinner until it has the consistency of heavy cream or of honey (Fig. 103), or by means of a plastic ring pressed into the hole with the cloth, from the outside, but allowing some slack in the cloth (Fig. 103). When the cloth is attached to the lid with

Fig. 102. Cage for shipping a 2-pound package of bees.

putty, the putty must dry for at least 24 hours before use. The can is filled with sugar syrup and the lid is sealed to the can with a can sealer. When the plastic ring is used, the lids are sealed to empty cans after which the cans are filled and the cloth and ring installed. Friction top cans are seldom used because they are more subject to leakage of the syrup.

The syrup used as feed varies among shippers. Fifty-fifty sugar syrup made of one part granulated sugar and one part water has been satisfactory for many years. Most recently liquid sugar has supplanted the 50:50 granulated sugar syrup because of its convenience. It is bought in truck tank loads and is stored in large tanks near the warehouse workroom. The liquid sugar commonly used is known as Type 50 syrup and contains 77% solids of which 50% is invert sugar. This is diluted with water to bring the solids to 50%.

Filling the Packages

Package cages are filled in the apiaries directly from the colonies supplying the bees. Bulk bee boxes are not used unless the bees have been

Fig. 103.   a   b
Feed cans for package bee cages. Two types of feed hole closures: (a) cloth attached to inside of lid; (b) cloth attached to lid by plastic ring that holds the cloth in the feed hole.

bought as bulk bees from other beekeepers. In some cases bulk bees are accumulated in stacked bodies of honey and empty combs for filling package cages later.

The queens for the packages are caged in 2-hole queen cages directly from the mating nuclei and are without attendants or food. Soon after the queens are caged the cages with queens are fitted into special cage holding frames (Fig. 98), and are placed into carrying boxes stocked with young bees and provided with a comb of honey. They are transported to the apiaries in these. Frequently the caged queens will be held for a brief time in "queen banks," which are hives strong with queenless bees and provided with two or three combs of honey as food, or with empty combs for storing sugar syrup and fumagillin that is fed and for clustering.

The colonies that will supply bees for the packages have usually been over-wintered in two full depth brood bodies. The first bees shaken from them are used for cell builders. Bees are shaken from only the strongest

Fig. 104. Bees driven into top body of two-story colony preparatory to filling package cages.

colonies and the "take" from each colony is light. The bees may be shaken into package cages for distribution to cell builders, or into "bulk bee" boxes (Figs. 77 and 78) from which they are dipped for cell builders, or for establishment of nuclei, after having been sprayed lightly with 30:70 or 40:60 sugar syrup at least half an hour earlier. Before dipping, the bees should be clustered in the box and in such condition they can be dipped as a cohesive mass. The colonies from which bees are taken are fed 4:6 or 1:1 sugar syrup immediately after the bees are shaken from the colonies to encourage continued expansion of broodrearing.

The first packages are shipped in late March or early April. The yield of bees for the first shipments may average 5 to 6 pounds per colony, or sometimes higher. The second "shaking" about two weeks later may average 3 to 4 pounds of bees per colony, and subsequent shakings about the same. About half the bees are removed from the colony at each shaking, though this may vary between shippers.

For many years the package cages were filled by the slow method of finding the colony queen and setting her between two combs outside

Fig. 105. Early model "shaker box" consisting of three full depth hive bodies. The two lower ones have combs, and the upper one is empty with an excluder attached to its bottom.

of the colony and then shaking the bees from part of the remaining combs through a funnel into a package cage resting on scales. Drones were included with the bees, which displeased some customers. Some bee-keepers eliminated the drones from packages by confining the queen and brood to the lower of two full depth bodies by excluders. Part of the bees are driven into the body above the excluder by removing the hive top and smoking the colony at the entrance (Fig. 104). No drones are among the bees shaken from the top body, and it is not necessary to find the queen each time bees are harvested.

A more flexible and faster system was later devised to eliminate drones from packages and to avoid the necessity of finding the queen each time before the packages are filled. This system makes use of a forerunner of the modern shaker box and it was called a "shaker box." To construct this box, two full depth bodies are prepared so that each will hold 5 or 6 combs evenly spaced. A ventilating screen is fastened to the bottom edge of one of the bodies. A third but empty body has an excluder attached to the bottom edge. The shaker box is set up so the body that is closed with the screen is the bottom body, then the other body with frames, and the empty body on top (Fig. 105). Bees are shaken into the top body of this shaker box from a body of the colony supplying the bees which had been placed on top of the shaker box. If the queen had been on one of the shaken combs, she could be found easily on the excluder and returned to her hive. Drones are sifted by the excluder from the bees to be packaged.

When the combs are thickly covered with bees (Fig. 106), the bees from one comb at a time are shaken or brushed through a funnel into a shipping cage until the proper weight is recorded on the scales. As soon as the required weight is reached, which usually is about ⅛ pound more than the designated weight of the bees in the filled package, the caged queen is hung by a metal tab attached near one end of the queen cage which is inserted in a slot in the top of the package cage and is bent over to secure the queen cage near the feed can. The feed can is then dropped into place.

This type of shaker box has been largely replaced by a light weight three piece shaker box without combs (Fig. 107). The upper part has a funnel to fit into the lower part and a deep removable excluder tray that fits into the deep rim of the funnel above. Bees from the colony are shaken onto the excluder from a body of the donor colony placed on the rim (Fig. 108), and are caught in the box below, excluding drones and also the queen should she have been on one of the shaken combs. When several pounds of bees are in the box, the cages are filled by pouring the bees from the lower section of the shaker box into a package cage on scales (Fig. 109). Care must be taken that an overabundance of bees is not accumulated in the shaker box before they are poured into cages because bees may become overheated.

Fig. 106. Early model shaker box loaded with bees ready for packaging.

Fig. 107. The modern shaker box is light and easily handled. The excluder tray is removable.

Fig. 108. Bees are shaken into the shaker box from a body of the donor colony placed on top of the shaker box.

For the first and sometimes second harvest of bees, or shaking, some beekeepers place an excluder over the top body of colonies to be shaken and above that a specially designed box the size of a 6⅝" deep super but having cross partitions spaced about 2 inches apart, and a screened top (Fig. 110). The hives are smoked at the entrance to drive part of

Fig. 109. Package cages are filled by pouring bees from the collecting portion of the shaker box through a funnel into a package cage resting on scales.

Fig. 110. Some beekeepers smoke the bees up through an excluder placed over the top body and into a shallow body screened on top and having cross partitions for the bees to cling to.

Fig. 111. The partitioned "catcher box" with bees is set onto the shaker box from which the excluder has been removed, and the bees are jarred into the shaker box.

the bees into the special box where they adhere to the partitions. The box with bees is now set on the rim of the shaker box, the excluder tray having been removed, and by a sharp jolt the bees are made to tumble through the funnel into the holding box below (Fig. 111).

Recently a weighing container was devised to assist in accurate measuring of bees. Two containers of equal weight are used with each scale in use. While one container is being filled on the scale, the other is emptied into a package cage (Fig. 112).

Before shipment the packages must be "crated" if more than one package are shipped together. For shipment of individual packages an 8" or 9" lath is sometimes nailed at the bottom of each end. For truck shipments, four or five packages are fastened together with two 40" strips of lath, leaving a 2½" space between each package when five packages are crated together, and about 6" when the crate consists of four packages (Fig. 113). In most cases the cages are fastened together after they are filled because it is necessary to weigh each package during filling. The use of the weighing container that has come into use permits the cages to be crated in the warehouse before they are filled because the bees are

Fig. 112. Two weighing baskets of equal weight are used to fill precrated cages.

Fig. 113. Filled cages must be crated for shipment.

Fig. 114. A "jig" facilitates crating packages so the cages are evenly spaced.

Fig. 115. Colonies from which bees were taken are fed after shaking.

Fig. 116. For large scale feeding, pressure tanks with sugar syrup may be transported on a truck to the yards. One hose with a cut-off valve makes filling the syrup containers fast and easy.

weighed before they are put in the cage. In either case, crating is facilitated by using a "jig" to properly space the package cages (Fig. 114). Colonies from which bees are taken are fed 1:1 sugar syrup before leaving the yard (Figs. 115 and 116).

Elimination of Bees Adhering to the Outside of the Cages

Bees shipped by parcel post must have no bees whatever adhering to the outside of the cages. Bees shipped by truck are often held in an air conditioned room or other cool darkened place while the truckload of bees is being accumulated. Many of the bees adhering to the outside of the package cages are often lost in transit from the apiary to the storage area. Others may fly to lighted areas of the storage room, or to screened vents.

A few bees on the outside of cages transported by truck is of no consequence. However, bees present in quantity can interfere with ventilation

Fig. 117. "Hitch hiking" bees must be removed from the screens of package cages before shipment. Some beekeepers use a "brushing box" to catch bees brushed from the cages.

of the packages and must be eliminated. A brushing box (Fig. 117) to eliminate the "hitchhikers" was formerly commonly used, and is still used by some package shippers. Other shippers remove bees adhering to the cages with a shop vacuum cleaner.

Feeding Before Shipment

Some of the package bee producers spray the screens of the cages lightly one time with 40:60 sugar syrup while they are held before shipping. Some others prefer to spray lightly with water which aids in cooling the bees and induces them to cluster and remain quiet as well as furnishing water to the bees.

Installation

Package bees represent a considerable investment by the purchaser and they should be properly installed and cared for.

Upon receipt, the packages should be put in a cool darkened place and the screens of the cages sprayed lightly with 40:60 sugar syrup having Fumidil B. This may be repeated an hour later. When the bees are dry, and in the afternoon after 4 p.m., in the moonlight, or in the morning before 10 a.m., the bees are installed. It is best to install the bees at a time or temperature when they would not normally fly. The packages are taken to the apiary location and are protected from sun, wind, and rain or snow while awaiting installation. Three or four combs are withdrawn from the middle of each prepared hive that is already on location. A division board feeder or other feeder is filled with syrup. The entrances of the hives should be reduced, and if robbing is a problem, robber screens should be used.

Unless the temperature in the apiary is low enough to chill dampened bees in the hive, a package is now mist sprayed lightly with water or thin sugar syrup to reduce flying but not cause the bees to be sticky, and the bees are jolted to the bottom of the cage. The feed can and queen are removed and the bees are poured from the cage into the hive. The bees are leveled out on the bottom board with a hive tool and the frames replaced, letting them settle by their own weight. The cork is removed from the bee entry hole of the queen cage and the cage with the queen is inserted between two frames to allow the queen to emerge from the cage. This procedure is preferable to spraying the caged queen and dropping her from the cage onto the mass of bees where she could be injured when the frames are replaced. The cover is replaced, preferably with a temporary burlap "inner cover."

A two-queen colony may be established at the same time. After installation of the bees below, a "divide board" with a 7 x 10 inch center opening excludered on both sides is placed over the lower body with the entrance toward the front. Screen is laid over the center opening of the divide board, and paper over that. A second body is placed on the divide board, a division board feeder filled with sugar syrup, and three combs removed from the middle. One pound of bees and a queen are installed, a temporary inner cover of burlap is put over the body, and the hive cover replaced.

When the upper queen is laying, the paper and screen are removed so the heat from the larger colony below will help the smaller colony develop. The burlap is removed after the weather becomes warmer. The top colony may later be placed on a bottom board and transported to another apiary to be operated as a single queen colony if two-queen colonies are not desired. The advantage of this system is that three pounds of bees instead of four are used to establish two colonies.

The "direct release" method of package bee installation described above is one of the best, though other methods of installing packages are preferred by some beekeepers, and those methods are described in books and bee journals.

CHAPTER VII

Stock Maintenance and Improvement by Beekeepers

Many dedicated beekeepers are interested in the quality of their bees, that is, how well the bees meet the requirements the beekeeper somehow associates with his conception of the "ideal" bee. As we know, honey bees, like other organisms, vary in many respects. Individual bees may differ in color, size, temper, industry, and in other ways. Colonies, composed of individual bees, reflect the characteristics of the bees themselves, and lines, strains, or stocks to which the colonies belong are in turn characterized by their component colonies. Though often the practical differences between colonies or lines are minor, or are of such a nature they are unnoticed, in other cases significant differences are readily apparent, and it is these latter differences that prompt beekeepers to consider the quality of their bees with the objective of maintaining lines that please them or to improve those that are unsatisfactory.

What constitutes "good" stock and what constitutes "improvement" is a matter of opinion based as much upon individual likes and dislikes as upon solid evidence of the worth of a particular strain of bees. A bee-keeper's opinion is also influenced by his method of beekeeping, and sometimes by his geographical location.

Many queen breeders in the past were fortunate in having obtained excellent foundation stock; and by careful selection of queen mothers they were able to maintain the characteristics of the strain for many years, often until the queen breeder was no longer producing queens for sale. Occasionally, a colony was discovered that produced an enormous amount of honey, and for a brief time the mother of the colony was accorded fame and her daughters were widely distributed. These queens are now forgotten, and the lines that originated from them soon disappeared as victims of circumstances beyond the queen breeder's control.

We realize today that the obstacles faced by queen breeders of only a few years ago were so overwhelming it is a cause for wonder that their efforts attained the success they did. Control of mating was at best haphazard, except in those instances where isolation of the mating yards was unusually good. That the virgin queen mates with more than one drone was considered an anomaly. Genic control of sex and its effect on brood viability was unknown until comparatively recently. Knowledge of genetics and breeding had not yet been applied to bees, and colony descriptions necessary for colony evaluations and comparison were inadequate. It is with the benefit of new knowledge and techniques that the beekeeper today can look with confidence on the bright probability of the development and maintenance of strains of bees that are exceptionally well suited to his needs and desires.

This should not be taken, however, as encouragement for beekeepers in general to devote much time and effort in attempting to breed better bees. Bee breeding is, indeed, a highly specialized and technical aspect of beekeeping. It is best accomplished by those who have the training and experience necessary for the work, and who will perform research and development in commercial bee breeding centers or in university or government laboratories.

Beekeepers can, nevertheless, maintain good stock in many cases, and even bring about some desirable changes in their stock if they are willing to make the necessary effort. It is beyond the purpose of this chapter to do more than present a minimum of practical basic knowledge a beekeeper should have to make his breeding efforts worthwhile and help him avoid the pitfalls that are inherent in a maintenance or improvement program. Anyone seriously interested in attempting to breed bees should become familiar with published material on the subject, and extend his knowledge of genetics and breeding as much as is feasible.

Maintenance of the Characteristics of a Stock

To keep a stock "pure" is beyond the ability of most beekeepers, but traits that characterize a particular stock may be retained in the stock even though queens may mate with some drones of other stocks. Thus it is more accurate to speak of maintaining the characteristics of a stock rather than its purity.

Hobby beekeepers with a few colonies of bees which are within twice the flying distance to colonies of other lines may find it is difficult, if not impossible, to keep the same characteristics in the bees year after year. The most practical way in such cases to assure similar bees continuously is to secure replacement queens from the queen breeder who furnished the stock originally.

On the other hand, beekeepers with several hundred or more colonies of bees from which to select breeding queens may find it possible to maintain the characteristics of their stock, if drones of the stock are provided in abundance, even though colonies of other stocks are within easy flight range of the queen rearing colonies.

One basic reason for this is that, though queens mate with several drones, if proper drones are plentiful, queens will, in some cases at least, mate with drones that are most or all from the beekeeper's stock. By careful selection of queen mothers on the basis of their colony performance and the extent to which the queens, their drones, and their colonies conform to the beekeeper's stock, those queens that have mated entirely or mostly with drones of their own stock will likely be chosen as breeding queens.

Maintenance of stock is not without its hazards, and the beekeeper must be alert to these. One of the most common and most serious is loss of sex genes of the sex allelic series. To avoid this loss, several breeding queens that were *not used as such the year before* should be selected each year to be mothers of the queens that are reared to requeen the beekeeper's colonies. Requeening a large proportion of colonies with daughters of a favorite breeding queen, and the use of the same breeding queen the following year may, if routinely practiced, bring about a deterioration of brood solidness due to the two sex alleles in some of the fertilized eggs being alike. When the sex alleles are alike the larva that hatches from such an egg is male instead of female (Mackensen 1951; Rothenbuhler 1957; Woyke 1963a) and is eaten by the worker bees, leaving an empty cell among the cells of the brood comb.

Improvement of Stock by the Beekeeper

While successful maintenance of good stock requires considerable experience in practical beekeeping, and careful observation and discriminating selection of parents of the next generation, stock improvement, other than introduction of good stock of other lines, demands in addition some knowledge of the biology and behavior of bees, and how traits in general are inherited, as well as an acquaintance with peculiarities of honey bee inheritance. Fortunately, most characteristics of bees that are of interest to beekeepers are variable and, assuming at least some control over the mating of the queens, can probably be changed in some degree by selection to intensify the desirable traits and minimize the undesirable ones. One should bear in mind, however, that mere change is not necessarily improvement.

Colony Descriptions or Profiles

Beekeepers, as a rule, judge their colonies by experience, commonly known as "eyeballing," and select those for breeders that appear to have the traits they want in their bees that are more pronounced than those displayed by the majority of the colonies in the apiary. This has actually worked very well in many cases in maintenance of stock, even in the absence of strict control of mating. It may be the best most beekeepers can do, and when combined with provision of an abundance of drones from carefully selected drone mothers, the results can be satisfactory for stock maintenance.

If a stock is to be improved, on the other hand, colonies must be described more accurately and completely, and in terms that remain constant in meaning and establish bases on which to make judgments. Such descriptions may be called "profiles." Without profiles there is no reliable basis for colony comparison nor for determining the results of selection and breeding efforts. In addition, beekeeping practices must be such that test queens are fully developed, and each test colony must have an equal opportunity to develop and produce to its maximum potential in the test environment.

There is no one correct way to describe colonies for breeding purposes; each person will devise his own system. Nevertheless, it may be helpful to start with a system that has been used with satisfaction by others. Some kind of record of queen and colony parentage, characteristics, and performance is essential if the beekeeper is to control his program; and the descriptions should be clear, concise, reasonably accurate, relatively easily made, quickly understood, and truly descriptive. To this might be added flexibility for various approaches to analysis and use of the data. A "standardized" form for each colony for recording data in an immediately usable format is far superior to descriptive written notes in a notebook that must be reduced to summaries. Two such simplified forms and their use are discussed below: the individual queen record and the yard sheet.

Individual Queen Record

An individual record is kept for each queen and her colony to be described (Fig. 118). Certain entries do not change and are shown in the heading part of the form. A list of characteristics to be observed when appropriate and operations to be performed as needed is located to the left of the form. The main body of the form consists of a series of columns in which observations or manipulations are entered for the date they were made or performed. This record is kept in the office.

When the colonies are examined, data are recorded in the apiary on yard sheets (Fig. 119), similar to the individual queen record forms, and transferred later to the individual records for permanent filing.

BEE BREEDING PROGRAM
Individual Queen Record

Pg. ....

Mating .... Queen No. .... Colony No. ....

Emerged .... Clipped .... Marked .... From Nuc. ....

Established Colony ....

Observation or Manipulation	Date	Date	Date	Date	Date	Date	Date	Date	Date
NUMBER OF BODIES									
COLONY POPULATION									
TEMPER									
BROOD: amount									
: appearance									
DISEASE: afb									
: efb									
: sac									
: paralysis									
:									
WAX WORKING									
ENTER SUPERS									
SWARMING									
SUPERSEDURE									
HONEY REMOVED									
COMBS + or −									
FOUNDATION + or −									
HONEY STORES									
POLLEN STORES									

Notes: (over)

Fig. 118. Simplified form of an individual queen record. The data taken in the field and recorded on a yard sheet are transferred to the individual queen record form for permanent filing.

BEE BREEDING PROGRAM
Yard Sheet

....

Date Colonies Worked .... Pg. ....

Observation or Manipulation	Col. No.	Col. No.	Col. No.	Col. No.	Col. No.	Col. No.	Col. No.	Col. No.	Col. No.
NUMBER OF BODIES									
COLONY POPULATION									
TEMPER									
BROOD: amount									
: appearance									
DISEASE: afb									
: efb									
: sac									
: paralysis									
:									
WAX WORKING									
ENTER SUPERS									
SWARMING									
SUPERSEDURE									
HONEY REMOVED									
COMBS + or −									
FOUNDATION + or −									
HONEY STORES									
POLLEN STORES									

Notes: (over)

Fig. 119. Yard sheet for use with the simplified individual queen record form. These sheets are taken to the field when the colonies are examined, and the data recorded on them are transferred to the individual queen records for permanent filing.

Mating. The identifying symbol of the *mother* of the queen heading the test colony and, if known, the symbols of the *mothers* of the drones to which the queen which heads the colony was mated are shown in the "mating" space of the individual queen record. For initial queens this space may be blank or show the source of the stock.

Queen number. Initial queens chosen for breeders should be given identifying numbers, letters, or a combination of numbers and letters and this identification is put in the queen number section. Subsequent queens would each be assigned a symbol that would identify a particular queen and would never be used again. It can be seen that lineage is traced through the queens because the drones are essentially reproductive cells of their mothers.

Colony number. Testing hives should be numbered so each can be positively identified.

Emerged. The date (month, day, and year) the queen emerged from the cell.

Clipped. The date the queen was clipped, and whether the left wings (L) or right wings (R).

Marked. If the queen is marked, give date and type or color of mark.

From Nuc. The number of the nucleus in which the queen is emerged or introduced should be given here with the date the cell or queen was put in the nucleus.

Established Colony. Initial colonies chosen for test or for breeders will already have been established and some appropriate entry such as "field colony" can be made here. Colonies to be tested that will be headed by daughters of initial queens that were selected as queen mothers should be established anew within a period of a day or two and as near alike as possible. It is suggested that they be made up with three pounds of bees, four combs of honey, one comb well filled with pollen, four or five empty combs, and no brood. These data, or any deviation from them, should be shown. For example: "4-10-78 3 lb. bees, 4 fr honey, ½ fr pollen, 4 combs. Intro. queen by push-in cage."

About 14 days after the test colonies are established the first ratings should be made, and thereafter ratings should be made at about 14-day intervals until the main honey flow. During the honey flow, it is advisable to discontinue all ratings except the amount of honey removed and the combs or foundation put on. After the honey flow all applicable ratings should be made as before and especially when the colony is prepared for winter.

In making observations and ratings, it is very important to base the ratings on the actual condition of the colony at the time of observation.

Make no allowances. If the bees are examined on a chilly day and they are "mean" they should be rated as mean in spite of the fact they may have been gentle on a better day. If there is something that should be mentioned, such as chilly weather, these comments can be made on the back of the yard sheet, along with any comments pertaining to individual hives. The comments can be associated with the proper hives by identifying them with the appropriate hive numbers.

Yard Sheet

The yard sheet (Fig. 119) has a list of observations or manipulations arranged in a column at the left side of the sheet. Across the page to the right there is a series of blank columns each of which is headed at the top by a space for a colony number. The ratings, observations, or manipulations are written into the proper spaces of the columns. If at any examination no observation is made of a particular character, or a particular manipulation is not made, the space pertaining to the item is left blank. Rating entries should be understandable at a glance, such as numbers or abbreviations that signify a particular degree of a behavioral character: 5 = ex (excellent); 4 = vg (very good); 3 = g (good); 2 = f (fair); and 1 = po (poor). Superscripts + and – can indicate the top and bottom fourth or third of a class, if desired. The amount of brood, bees, honey, or pollen is best expressed in absolute numbers, as frames with brood or bees, and pounds or frames of honey, and frames or square inches of pollen. At the end of the season these can be converted to the 1 to 5 rating system if a single composite index is desired for each queen.

An explanation of the ratings is given below:

Number of Bodies. The number of bodies (broodnest and supers) *before* the colony is worked is entered each time.

Colony Population. Number of frames at least fairly well covered with bees. If outer combs have only a few bees, do not include them. Disregard bees on sides of hive and on bottom board.

Temper. Use following ratings: 5 or ex = very gentle; 4 or vg = gentle; 3 or g = usual docility; 2 or f = more touchy than usual; 1 or po = mean; and O or vpo (very poor) = vicious.

Brood: amount. Number of frames with brood. When outer frames have only a small amount, either omit them or estimate as a part frame. No brood observations during the honey flow.

Brood: appearance. 5 or ex = a solid appearance with very few empty cells among the sealed brood (0 to 3 empty cells per 100 cells); 4 or vg = 4 to 7 empty cells per 100 cells; 3 or g = usual number of empty cells (8-11 per 100 cells) and compact appearing brood; 2 or f = 12-20 empty cells per 100 cells; 1 or po = many empty cells among sealed cells (over 20 per 100 cells).

Disease. No entry is made unless disease appears during test period. 2 or hvy (heavy) = badly infected; 3 or mod (moderate) = moderately infected; 4 or lgt (light) = light infection; 5 = no infection. Identify the disease, if present.

Wax Working. 5 or ex = draw foundation rapidly; 4 or vg = draw foundation moderately rapidly and evenly; 3 or g = draw foundation slowly and evenly; 2 or f = draw foundation very slowly and/or unevenly; 1 = neglect or destroy foundation.

Enter Supers. 5 or ex = occupy supers readily; 4 or vg = occupy supers moderately readily; 3 or g = occupy supers somewhat slowly; 2 or f = occupy supers slowly; 1 or po = occupy supers very slowly or not at all.

Swarming. 5 or ex = do not swarm even when crowded; 4 or vg = swarm when crowded, but respond to manipulation and room; 3 or g = swarm when crowded, do not respond to added room and moderate manipulation after swarm cells are started; 2 or f = swarm before crowded; 1 or po = swarm when weak.

Supersedure. 5 or ex = do not supersede within 24 months; 4 or vg = supersede between 12 and 24 months; 3 or g = supersede between 6 and 12 months; 2 or f = supersede between 3 and 6 months; 1 or po = supersede in less than 3 months.

Honey Removed. The supers should be marked so each can be identified. Weigh them "on" and "off," that is, weigh them before putting on the colony and again after they are removed. The difference in weight is the honey removed. A less accurate estimate can be made by recording the number of frames of honey removed. Frames of honey removed from the broodnest should be recorded.

Combs + or -. Record the number of empty combs, or nearly so, added to or removed from the colony at the time the colony is examined.

Foundation + or -. Record the number of frames of foundation which are added, or removed as foundation or partially drawn combs. If fully drawn out, record as comb removed.

Honey Stores. Frames of honey in broodnest. If colony is fed syrup, record amount of syrup, and give formula on back of record form. If fed honey in frames, record number of full frames. No observation during main honey flow. When a colony is ready for winter, weigh hive, or estimate amount of honey in frames.

Pollen Stores. If pollen is fed to the colony, give the amount. If in combs, estimate the number of full frames or square inches. If in cakes, give the weight of the cake and on the reverse side of the form explain the composition of the cake. No observation during the main honey flow.

When the colony is prepared for winter, estimate the amount of pollen in the hive. Usually, combs will be only partially filled with pollen. The amount of pollen in partially filled combs can be totaled and expressed as "frames" or as square inches. A "full frame" consists of both sides of a comb from near the top bar to the bottom bar and to near both end bars.

Biological Phenomena Underlying Bee Breeding

It has been mentioned that bees differ: races; strains within a race; colonies; and bees within a colony. These differences are due largely to differences in heredity. Environmental variables are not excluded as influencing variability of bees, but the responses to environmental differences are conditioned by the genotypes of the individuals. The genotype is the complicated organization of certain specific substances in the cell nucleus, called genes, that are passed from parent to offspring by means of the reproductive cells and which, in coordination with various elements of the environment, direct the formation of individuals and their functioning.

To understand the reasons for various breeding practices, it is necessary to know something about the reproductive cells, their origin and function, and the hereditary material, or genes, which they carry.

Origin and Maturation of Eggs

The queen's reproductive cells are eggs. They originate from special cells, the oogonia, in the anterior closed ends of cellular tubes, the ovarioles, which make up the major part of the paired ovaries (Fig. 2). After they originate they are called oocytes, and begin to move toward the posterior ends of the ovarioles which open into the anterior ends of the lateral oviducts. As they traverse the ovarioles each is joined behind by a group of nurse cells that also originated in the closed ends of the ovarioles, and from the same oogonium that gave rise to the oocyte. Both the oocyte and the group of nurse cells become enclosed in separate but connected chambers of a cellular envelope (Fig. 3). They enlarge by accumulation of cell substance, the nurse cells growing more rapidly than the oocyte. When they near the posterior ends of the tubules the oocyte suddenly consumes the nurse cells and reaches its full size, after which the cells of the cellular envelope secrete a flexible egg shell or chorion. The "ripe" egg now passes from the ovariole into a lateral oviduct where several may accumulate awaiting deposition in the comb.

At this point the egg is fully formed, but it is not capable of developing into a female or male bee. It must first undergo a process of maturation which takes place about the time the egg is laid. The egg as it is forming has the hereditary material within its nucleus, which is a small spherical body in the egg enclosed within a membrane. This hereditary material is organized in minute bodies known as chromosomes. Chromosomes in the newly formed egg exist as pairs. One of each pair came from the mother of the queen producing the egg and the other from the father of the queen. There are 16 pairs of chromosomes, or two sets, a total of 32, in the developing egg, and also in the body cells of the queen herself. Though chromosomes are discrete bodies they are recognizable as such only briefly during times of cell division or maturation. Between such times they appear as a network in the nucleus.

It is apparent that since eggs that will develop into female bees are fertilized by sperm that themselves carry contributary chromosomes, the number of chromosomes in the egg must be systematically reduced before the egg is fertilized if the chromosome number is to remain constant. This is accomplished by two nuclear divisions in the egg. At the first division the members of each pair of chromosomes come together side by side. One member of the pair had come from the mother of the queen producing the egg and the other member came from her father. At this time the paired chromosomes may exchange segments, which is known as crossing over, and they then move away from each other to opposite ends of a spindle of contractile fibrils. It is a matter of chance which member of a pair goes to a particular end of the spindle, and which member of other pairs accompany it, so that all possible combinations of chromosomes that originated from the mother of the queen and the chromosomes that originated from her father will occur in different eggs. It is significant that each group of chromosomes has only one of each of the pairs, never two of one pair and none of another. Each group is therefore a complete set, but the sets in different matured eggs of a queen may have different combinations of chromosomes and thus of genes. It follows, then, that queens produce many genetically different kinds of eggs.

The chromosomes at the two ends of the spindle are now seen to have duplicated themselves and a second spindle is formed that brings about a separation of the duplicates that results in four new nuclei, each with one complete set of 16 chromosomes. Three of the nuclei, known as polar bodies, degenerate leaving one to survive as the egg pronucleus.

Origin and Maturation of Spermatozoa

The male sex cells, the spermatozoa, originate in the closed ends of the tubules of the testes from special cells. The future sperm cells, known at this stage as spermatogonia, become enclosed in a cellular cyst and after a number of multiplying divisions they attempt to undergo two maturation divisions. The first of these aborts and the second yields two cells with unequal amounts of cytoplasm in which the nucleus is suspended. The smaller one disintegrates. The larger one develops into a sperm with a head containing the choromosomes, and a vibratory tail to propel the sperm.

The drones develop from unfertilized eggs that have undergone maturation and thus like matured eggs from which they originated have one complete set of 16 chromosomes. They are spoken of as being haploid. It follows that spermatozoa which the drones produce not only have one complete set of chromosomes like matured eggs, but all sperm produced by one drone are identical. This fact is of crucial importance in bee genetics and breeding.

Normally a drone may produce about ten million spermatozoa. During development all of these are at the same stage at the same time. When they are completely formed they move to the seminal vesicles where they remain until the drone mates, and the testes degenerate to become amorphous bits of tissue applied to the anterior end of the seminal vesicles. The drone makes all of his sperm at one time and injects all of them into the queen at mating. A drone, therefore, can mate with only one queen, whereas a queen will mate with many drones on her mating flight or flights.

Functioning or Expression of Genes

The genes which a female bee receives from her mother and from her father, and the genes the drone received from his mother determine, under the influence of a particular environment, the kind of bee that emerges and how the bee will behave and react to the stimuli that impinge upon it. This is a complicated system. Different genes may function in different ways; and the same genes may be expressed differently in queens, workers, and drones due to internal and external environmental differences. The expression of a gene, which is the result of gene action, may be simple and straightforward, or it may exhibit various degrees of complexity. A single gene may be influenced by another, but non-allelic, gene to change the character produced. One allele may exert a stronger influence than its mate and be dominant, and genes at various loci may supplement each other so as more genes are present the effect on the character is intensified. Alleles may each produce different end products, and two different alleles when in the same bee may produce a character unlike that produced by either allele itself. For instance, the gene *snow* which produces white eyes and its allele *tan* which produces tan eyes when together in the same female bee produce red eyes. The same relationship may exist between non-allelic genes.

Perhaps one of the better known allelic interactions that is most important to beekeepers is the one involved in sex determination. Females are diploid; that is, they have two sets of chromosomes. On a particular chromosome of each set there is a specific place or locus where a gene involved in sex determination is situated. When the sex genes are different, that is are alleles, the bee is female and is said to be heterozygous for that particular locus. If the sex genes are alike, the sex of the bee is male, but the larva is eaten by workers soon after it hatches from the egg. Such a larva is homozygous for the sex alleles. If an egg is unfertilized a normal male will develop. A simplified explanation is that the differing alleles of a heterozygote interact to override the effect of male determining genes that may be present in the other chromosomes.

A familiar example will illustrate also the power of the environment to drastically influence the action of genes, rather than merely the genes influencing each other. The fertilized egg has the potential of becoming a queen or a worker, and whichever path it takes it has the same genotype. In female caste determination there is some environmental element involved that is different in the development of queens and of workers, and it causes certain genes to act, rather than others, or it changes the timing of gene action, or the sequence of gene action, so that the proper caste is formed.

These examples serve to underscore the complexity of how genes act and that simply crossing two good lines will not necessarily immediately result in a bee that combines the good characteristics of both lines.

Relationships of Individuals Within a Colony

One more complexity of the bee colony should be mentioned, and that is the unusual relationships of the individuals of the colony to one another.

The Queen. The honey bee colony is an operational unit to the beekeeper. To the bee breeder it is also a family, and like many families, it has two generations. The queen is diploid and is the mother of the workers and drones; but unlike most other mothers she functions also as a surrogate father because she has stored within her body the spermatozoa she acquired from her mates and she uses these to fertilize the eggs as she lays them. After she begins to lay, a queen does not mate again, and she never mates in the hive; she thus avoids mating with her mother's drones or her own.

The Workers. The workers are daughters of the queen, normally non-reproductive, and have both a mother and a father. They are the next generation and are diploid like their mother. They have two sets of chromosomes with 16 chromosomes in each set. Though they are like their mother in being diploid, they are not genetically the same as their mother because each has only a sample of her mother's heredity and has, in addition, heredity derived from her father which her mother does not have. The queen and the worker form two female castes, one of which has a reproductive function and one of which does not.

The Drones. The drones are the sons; but they are not truly sons even though they are male. They do not belong to either the parental or filial generations. They are intercalary between parental and filial generations because they are biologically sex cells, or gametes, of their mother since they originate from unfertilized matured eggs which are their mother's sex cells or gametes. By the formation of spermatozoa a drone changes the sex cell from which he arose from a single female sex cell, the matured egg with one set of 16 chromosomes, into millions of male sex cells each with the same one set of chromosomes. The sperm of a drone are therefore genetically identical with each other and with the egg that gave rise to the drone.

Through the mechanism of egg maturation a queen will produce many genetically different kinds of eggs and thus many genetically different kinds of drones, each of which is a sample of his mother's heredity, but each drone produces only one kind of sperm.

The drones of a colony are not the fathers of the worker bees in their colony. They are potential fathers of future colonies in that they will be intermediary in the transfer of genetic material from their mother to the virgin queens with which they mate. It follows that neither are they true brothers to the workers of their colony because the workers have a father while the drones do not. A drone simply represents a matured sex cell of his mother, and genetically when a drone mates with a queen the mating is, in effect, a mating between the drone's mother and the virgin queen. This fact leads to some interesting relationships between the female progeny of a queen which can vary with the source of the drones that mated with the queen.

The following examples may help to illustrate this point:

Queen mated to one drone. Such a mating would be rare in nature but is often made by instrumental insemination for specific purposes in the study of bee genetics and breeding.

The females, resulting from this mating (Fig. 120) have the same mother and father and are sisters. Each of them received a sample of

QUEEN MATED TO ONE DRONE

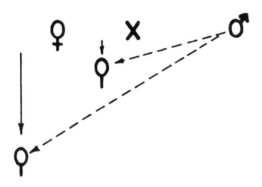

Fig. 120. Queen mated to one drone. Female progeny are all super sisters. (From Laidlaw, Apiacta, 1974)

her mother's heredity and they all received identical heredity from their father. This is unusual. Most diploid organisms receive a sample of heredity from both mother and father. These sisters are more closely related than full sisters and might be called *super* sisters.

Queen mated to several drones from different mothers. Queens nearly always mate with several drones. The sperm are mixed and stored in the spermatheca. As the eggs are laid some are fertilized with different sperm and some with identical sperm, that is, with sperm from different drones or sperm from the same drone (Fig. 121). When a queen mates with several drones, part of her female progeny will have different fathers. Each father will sire a subfamily, and the members of one subfamily, while super sisters to each other, will be half sisters of the members of the other subfamilies if the queen's mates had different mothers. This is the usual situation with open mated queens.

Queen mated to several drones from the same mother. This is a second type of mating that would be unlikely to occur in nature, but it is routine in the laboratory. It gives super sisters and full sisters (Fig. 122), but no half sisters.

QUEEN MATED TO TWO OR MORE DRONES
DRONES FROM DIFFERENT MOTHERS

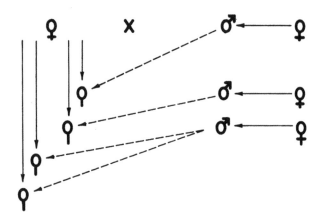

Fig. 121. Queen mated to two or more drones from different mothers. All females sired by one drone are super sisters, and females sired by different drones are half sisters. (From Laidlaw, Apiacta, 1974)

Since sex cells of a drone are genetically sex cells of his mother just as the eggs are, mating a queen to a drone is genetically the same as mating her to the drone's mother. In this case the drones all had the same mother and were all genetically gametes of the same queen. Each drone sires a subfamily, the members of which are super sisters, but the members of one subfamily are full sisters to the members of the other subfamilies because the genetic father of the bees is the mother of the drones, as strange as that may seem.

Queen mated to drones from several mothers and also to some drones having the same mother. In natural mating most queens would probably mate with drones having different mothers. In some cases a queen might mate with drones from different mothers and also some drones having the same mother. In this case (Fig. 123), the female progeny of the queen would consist of super sisters, full sisters, and half sisters.

Significance of honey bee relationships. An awareness of the relationships that can exist in a colony of bees, and of the subtleties these relationships introduce into bee breeding, can be helpful to the beekeeper in understanding the hereditary composition of colonies. However, the ac-

QUEEN MATED TO TWO OR MORE DRONES

DRONES FROM SAME MOTHER

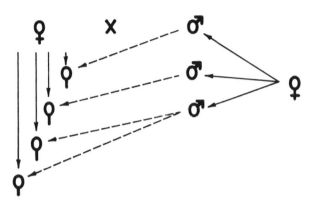

Fig. 122. Queen mated to two or more drones from the same mother. All females sired by one drone are super sisters, and females sired by different drones are full sisters. (From Laidlaw, Apiacta, 1974)

tual operation of a breeding program would no doubt be guided by the usual principles of population genetics.

It seems probable that in an undefined but restricted period of time the female progeny produced by a multiply mated queen may be predominantly super sisters sired by one drone, because sperm of a drone tend to remain together as "islands" in areas of the spermatheca (Taber 1955) and thus, for a time, a large proportion of identical sperm could be withdrawn by the queen to fertilize successive eggs as they are laid.

The queen herself is responsible for most of the variability of the workers of the colony because her mature eggs, or gametes, represent the full range of genetic combinations she is capable of producing. Her mates each produce only one kind of sperm and thus one genetic combination and the variability the mates introduce to the colony is limited to their number.

Beekeeper Management of Test Colonies

Beekeeper effort to improve stock must avoid, to the greatest extent possible, pitfalls inherent in stock testing. Some of the things that can

QUEEN MATED TO DRONES FROM DIFFERENT
MOTHERS AND ALSO DRONES FROM SAME MOTHER

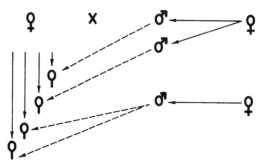

Fig. 123. Queen mated to drones from different mothers and also from the same mother. All females sired by one drone are super sisters. All sired by different drones from the same mother are full sisters, and all sired by different drones from different mothers are half sisters. (From Laidlaw, Apiacta, 1974)

obscure colony behavior and performance and thus bias the data are obvious, others may be overlooked.

Initial colonies for the program should be chosen with great care. At *least* five or ten queen mothers and ten to fifteen drone mothers should be selected as parents of the next generation so that loss of sex alleles will be averted. By rearing queens from each of the queen mothers for requeening the test colonies and open mating them to drones from the drone mothers, the sex alleles should be retained in the population (Woyke 1976).

The parents of the next generation should again be chosen with great care; and no less than five to ten should be designated as queen mothers and ten to fifteen as drone mothers. This procedure is followed each subsequent generation.

The critical selection of parents each generation tends to retain the genes responsible for the characteristics desired, and the use of a large number of queen mothers and drone mothers ensures that a maximum number of sex alleles will remain in the population throughout many generations.

If it should develop that daughters from only two or three queen mothers are selected as breeding queens for the next season, it might be advisable to add a daughter from two or three more queen mothers as breeding queens to further ensure the retention of sex alleles in the population.

Often the initial colonies chosen for the program will be established field colonies that display characteristics and performances that attract the attention of the beekeeper. Subsequent generations from these colonies must be managed from the outset so that the inherent qualities of the colonies are tested and are not distorted by different environmental influences.

One of the first concerns should be to rear virgins for testing that are fully developed queens. They should be the best queens it is possible to rear from the particular queen mother.

A second concern is to provide an overabundance of drones from selected drone mothers that hopefully will mate with the virgins. The drones should be reared from ten to fifteen, or more, drone mothers so loss of sex alleles will be minimized. The drone mother colonies should be given care comparable to that given queen mother colonies and cell builders to ensure that the drones will be reared when needed, cared for by the bees, and each will produce a copious amount of semen.

It is essential that each test queen be identified and marked so that any replacement of the queen, such as by supersedure or swarming, can be detected. Each time the broodnest is examined a cursory glance of the brood combs should be made for queen cells, and not only active cells removed but also any that have emerged or been torn down. Such cells alert one to the probability a virgin has emerged and if left may be misleading at later examinations.

All test colonies should have an equal start: in bees, honey, and pollen. Each test yard should have queens from each of the queen mothers because the environmental conditions of yards vary, and unless representatives of a "standard" line, which we do not have at present, are in each yard for comparison, the validity of test colony comparisons is doubtful. In addition, the colonies should be arranged in the yard to minimize or eliminate drifting.

Good beekeeping should be practiced so each colony can reach its full potential in its apiary. Each colony should receive the individual attention it requires, and notes made of what is done. There should always be adequate room for brood rearing and for nectar ripening and honey storage.

In the fall each colony should be put in the proper condition for wintering, and notes made of what was done. In the spring each colony should again receive the attention it needs, and notes made of conditions and of operations performed.

Admittedly, such a program requires a great deal of work. Unfortunately there is no simple way to improve bees, in contrast to simply maintaining good stock. If the beekeeper has a good knowledge of breeding theory, and uses instrumental insemination, the probability of achieving satisfactory results is enhanced.

CHAPTER VIII

A Brief History of Queen Rearing in the United States

When we become familiar with a subject there is a natural inclination to know something about its ancestry, and how the various early ideas about it, and its methods, evolved into present day practices. This, of course, is history.

But history can be humbling. As we delve into history it is not unusual to learn with surprise, and sometimes with chagrin, that at least the main element of what we think is a superb idea, outstanding discovery, or modern invention, was known many years earlier and was recorded in some publication. Queen rearing is no exception. Queen rearing today is fundamentally the same as that practiced in the latter part of the 1800's and early 1900's, but with adaptations to particular methods of beekeeping, economic requirements, and individual beekeeper preferences.

Bee Biology that is Basic to Queen Rearing

Queen and Worker Castes

We probably would be correct in beginning the history of contemporary queen rearing with Michel Jacob's discovery, published in 1568 (Townsend and Crane 1973), that worker bees can produce queens from very young larvae present in worker cells, a phenomenon that was rediscovered by Jansha 1770-1773 (Alphonsus 1931), and again by Schirach (1787). But this radical concept met with opposition. It was argued by dissenters that there must be some royal eggs in worker cells; and that workers were of a neuter sex so eggs that could develop into workers could not possibly develop into queens. Huber most effectively met these opposing opinions by innovative, simple, and carefully controlled experiments that showed queens can be reared from just-hatched to two-day old larvae in worker cells, thus proving that workers are females. This was further supported by Riem's discovery (Huber 1814) that workers may lay eggs that develop into drones, which Huber later confirmed by observations of his own. Even as early as the time of Charles Butler, Richard Remnant in his *Discourse or Historie of Bees* stated that workers are female (Townsend and Crane 1973). Miss Jurine, a friend of Huber, dissected many worker bees and found ovaries in all of them.

[*159*]

The discovery that larvae in worker cells can develop into queens is as important to queen rearing as Langstroth's recognition of the bee space is to beekeeping as a whole. All queen rearing methods under the control of the beekeeper are based upon it.

Aristotle, who lived 384 to 322 B.C., mentioned that some call the queen the mother of the colony. Apparently, Aristotle's casual statement had little effect on the thought of his time, or even much later, because the queen was still considered a king or general, in spite of the description in 1586 by Luiz Mendez de Torres (Townsend and Crane 1973) of the queen as a female that laid eggs, until Charles Butler published his thesis of 1609 that the queen was indeed a female. Supposedly she ruled the colony and was responsible for the origin of daughter queens. Swammerdam (1732) proved by anatomical studies that queens are female and drones male, and he thereby settled the question of the sex of the queen and drones, but he regarded workers as stunted males.

Jansha, Schirach, and Huber, who were contemporaries, were largely responsible for positively establishing the sex of worker bees, though Aristotle had stated that some beekeepers of his time affirm that drones are males and workers are females.

Schirach about 1771 (Huber 1814) supposed that larvae that became queens had been fed a special food which, in conjunction with a more spacious cell, brought about their development as queens. Huber with his characteristic fine perception stated that the very young larvae in worker cells are neither worker nor queen larvae, and until a larva is three days old it "contains alike the germs of the insect which shall prove industrious, and of the insect susceptible of fecundity."

In an attempt to discover how a worker or a queen could be produced from an egg deposited in a worker cell, von Planta analyzed larval food and published his data in 1848. He concluded that young queen and worker larvae are fed the same food for the first three days following hatching, and on the fourth day the food given to larvae that will become workers is changed by the addition of honey and pollen, but larvae to become queens continue to receive the same larval food as before. This explanation is essentially true, and it enjoyed unquestioning acceptance until later research indicated there is a special substance or combination of substances in larval food that is instrumental in female caste determination (Shuel *et. al.* 1978; Weaver 1955, 1956).

Beetsma (1979) presented evidence that higher sugar content of queen jelly induces larvae in queen cells to eat more than worker larvae, and this regulates the amount of juvenile hormone produced. Juvenile hormone is instrumental in caste differentiation. It is known that very young female larvae fed abundantly by the bees become excellent queens, while older larvae or larvae fed scantily fail to attain the same degree of differentiation. Huber expressed the idea that bees may occur that have a mixture of queen and worker characteristics and thus fall between the two extremes represented by queens and workers. Such forms do occur and are now known as intercastes.

Drones and Parthenogenesis

Charles Butler had referred to drones as males in 1609, and Swammerdam (1732) showed by his anatomical studies that drones are males. Swammerdam's work was convincing and there were few challenges to it, but the origin of drones became the subject of much speculation, most believing that drones develop from fertilized eggs, or as Huber stated, from special fertilized eggs that may occupy a special place in the ovaries, though he had some doubts about this. Huber found support for his conclusion, among other things, in that laying workers produced male eggs only, and thus laid only special eggs, and queens that mated later than 21 days following emergence laid "drone" eggs only.

It was Dzierzon in 1845 (Berlepsch 1861) who demonstrated by the use of two races of bees that could be visually identified that female bees arise from fertilized eggs and drones from unfertilized eggs. An Italian queen mated with black drones produced hybrid workers and pure Italian drones. The same phenomenon was observed when a pure black queen was mated to Italian drones; in this case also, the females were hybrid but the drones were pure black. Dzierzon reasoned from this that the eggs in the ovaries of a queen are not fertilized but become so as they are laid if they are to give rise to females. The queen possesses the ability to lay fertilized or unfertilized eggs at will and therefore controls the sex of her offspring. These facts are of fundamental importance to the bee breeder.

Drones and Fertilization of the Eggs

It is interesting that though the drones were shown to be males by Swammerdam, the way they functioned was not understood. No one had witnessed the mating of the queen, and Swammerdam thought there was no union between queen and drone but the eggs were fertilized by penetration of the queen's body by the odor of the drones, which he termed "aura seminalis," and not by the fluid in the "spherical sac," the spermatheca, which he believed provided the sticky substance of the end of the egg that attaches the egg to the cell bottom. It has been shown since then that the stickiness of the end of the egg is produced by the egg itself or by the follicular cells that encase the egg in the ovarioles.

Some beekeepers believed the drones fertilized the eggs by ejaculating semen upon the eggs the queen had deposited in the cells, and others were of the opinion that the workers determined the sex of the bees by the food furnished them. Still others considered the queen has no need to mate and that she can lay eggs that develop into females without her having mated. Even in the time of Huber, after it was shown that queens must mate in order to lay eggs that develop into females, the manner in which the eggs were fertilized was a mystery. Huber assumed the eggs were fertilized in the ovaries but found difficulty in explaining how eggs yet undeveloped could be fertilized. As we know now, worker bees of a race of honey bees in South Africa, *Apis mellifera capensis,* can lay unfertilized eggs that develop into females (Onions 1912), and that, rarely, virgin queens of our bees may lay eggs that develop into females (Mackensen 1943). Tucker (1958) has suggested an explanation for this.

The true explanation of the fertilization of the egg was given in 1784 by Posel (Langstroth 1913), who described the oviducts of the queen, the spermatheca and its contents, and the use of the sperm in fertilizing the eggs as they pass through the oviduct beneath the juncture of the spermathecal duct and the median oviduct. Posel may have been preceeded in his description by that of M. Audouin who discerned the true character of the spermatheca and provided an explanation of Jansha's observation that the semen received by a queen on a single mating flight was sufficient for her life (Leuckart 1861). Professor von Siebold in 1843 examined the spermatheca of a mated queen and found it filled with sperm which were available to fertilize the eggs, thus verifying the function of this organ.

The way the sperm are actually applied to the egg as it is laid remains a matter of conjecture. Many hypotheses have been advanced, but none have yet convincingly refuted that of Adam (1913) which holds that the valvefold presses the micropyle of the egg against the orifice of the spermathecal duct momentarily to allow one or more sperm to enter the bare protoplasm at the micropylar opening.

Mating of the Queen

Mr. de Reaumur in 1734-1742, along with others of his time, believed the queen mated in the hive. Reaumur tried to control the mating by enclosing a virgin in a glass box with several drones. Though this was unsuccessful, it probably represents the first attempt to control mating.

Anton Jansha (1771) discovered that the queen mates away from the hive. Huber about 20 years later, and unaware of Jansha's discovery, performed experiments that proved the queen never mates in the hive but always flies to mate. Incidentally, after this discovery, Huber, at Bonnet's suggestion, tried unsuccessfully to artificially inseminate queens by painting semen onto the vulva of the queen by means of a hair pencil, and was thus the first to attempt mating control by artificial insemination.

With the realization that the queen mates away from the hive, beekeepers began to devise methods to exercise at least some control over mating so their efforts at selection and breeding would be more successful. These methods all revolved around some kind of isolation that would exclude undesirable drones from having access to the queens. Among these were mating stations on plains, deserts, islands, or high in the mountains. These were moderately successful, and this method of mating control is still in use today.

Another, but later, method that found some degree of success was to confine the virgin and the drones it was desired that she mate with in a hive in a darkened and cool place until other drones had ceased flying (Ambroise 1924). The hive was then set outside and the entrance opened. Often the queen and drones would fly and mate, especially if the colony were fed some warm sugar syrup shortly before being set outside.

In spite of the sometimes satisfactory results of such methods, the desire to have full control over the queen's mating persisted. Queens and drones were confined to large enclosures of various kinds, but there were no verified matings in any of these, though claims of success were numerous.

Again the attention of some experimenters turned to artificial insemination. Since Huber's attempt, many others tried various ways to introduce semen into the queen, including eversion of the drone's copulatory organ into the sting chamber of the queen. There were undoubtedly some partial successes, but on the whole, the results were discouraging. The United States Department of Agriculture, recognizing the need for control of the queen's mating, appointed Nelson W. McLain to a position in the Department in 1885 for the purpose of developing a method of artificial insemination. While he did not succeed, he introduced the use of a syringe in transferring the semen from the drone to the queen. McLain, incidentally, was the first apiculturist employed by the United States government.

Zander (1911) and later Bishop (1920) found that when naturally mated queens return from the mating flight the oviducts are filled with semen. This fact was not emphasized by workers on artificial insemination until Laidlaw presented the results of his work in 1934 that queens artificially inseminated did not have semen in the oviducts because a flap-like obstruction in the vagina, the valvefold, prevented introduction of semen beyond it.

Watson (1926), though he overlooked the existence of the valvefold and its adverse influence, devised the first method of artificial insemination that was predictably, though partially, successful. He used a syringe, microscope, and lamp in the work, and appropriately called his method "instrumental insemination." Following him, Nolan, Laidlaw, Mackensen, and Roberts developed instrumental insemination to its present state. More recently, European workers, especially Ruttner, Vesely, and Woyke, and the South American workers, C. A. Camargo, J. M. F. Camargo, M. L. Mello, and L. S. Goncalves, have made contributions to the technique of insemination and to our understanding of queens and drones.

The disparity between the number of spermatozoa that reach the spermatheca of naturally mated and instrumentally inseminated queens was at first great. Watson, Nolan, and Mackensen had all found that inseminating with semen from several drones, or repeated inseminations, resulted in a greater number of sperm reaching the spermatheca. Nolan, and later Roberts, Oertel, and Tabor found that a considerable proportion of queens made more than one mating flight. Tryasko (1951) dissected queens immediately upon their return from their mating flight and discovered the oviducts contained more semen than one drone produces. There was, in fact, as much as is produced by 4 or 5 drones, or even more. Thus, a queen mates with several drones on a single mating flight, and this explains why instrumentally inseminated queens received more sperm in the spermatheca when they were inseminated with the semen from several drones, or were inseminated more than once. Tryasko's finding was verified by Tabor (1954). The fact that the queen mates with several drones and that she may mate with these on one flight has the greatest significance to the bee breeder.

Recognition by the Queen of Worker and Drone Cells

One more phenomenon that has interested beekeepers for centuries is the queen's laying eggs in worker cells that will produce workers, and eggs in drone cells that will produce drones, with rarely an error. Various hypotheses were advanced to explain this, but none were entirely convincing until Dr. N. Koeniger (1970) performed experiments that revealed that the queen measures the cells with her forelegs when she inspects them before she lays in them.

Emergence of Queen Rearing as a Beekeeping Practice

When bees were kept in boxes, hollow logs, and cylinders, rearing queen bees was not part of beekeeping activity, nor was it actually needed. Swarms were hived each year to replace colonies that died or were destroyed when the honey was harvested, or to increase the number of colonies in the apiary. They had their old queen with them, and a young queen soon took her place on the old stand. It was not until bees began to be "managed" and were kept in hives that permitted observation of activities of the colony and rearrangement or division of the combs and bees, that queen rearing became desirable. Nevertheless, before combs were situated in frames of one kind or another, or even attached to horizontal top bars, combs with brood were cut from hives and placed in other hives for colony increase. Part of the bees were "drummed" or smoked from the old hive to the new. Bees in the queenless part of such divisions reared their own queens.

The first "queen rearers" were beekeepers who were absorbed in the activities of their bees and who sought to understand them. Hives were designed that facilitated observation and experiment, and the need of queens for research arose. The two earliest methods of obtaining queens were use of swarm and supersedure cells, and division of a colony letting the queenless part rear a replacement queen (Schirach 1761, cited by Huber 1814; Jansha 1771, cited by Alphonsus 1931; Huber 1814, translated by C. P. Dadant 1926). These methods are still used today in a limited way and may be quite appropriate under certain circumstances. Though both are "primitive" methods, they are actually quite different. Queens from swarm or supersedure cells are reared by the bees from the beginning as queens, and bees' rearing of swarm cells is seasonal. Queens reared by queenless bees in divisions are started as a result of a beekeeper's interference with the colony, and such queens develop from larvae that originally were destined to become workers. Whether such queens are inferior to those emerging from swarm cells is a matter of disagreement among beekeepers, but there is little evidence that they are. Either method of obtaining a limited number of virgin queens may be a practical way for beekeepers with few colonies.

The next step forward in rearing queens was to get the bees to build queen cells when the beekeeper desired them and in the quantities needed. Jansha before 1771 (Alphonsus 1931) was certainly one of the first to devise a satisfactory method to accomplish this. He used a newly built comb with "hardly noticeable" larvae. The edge of the comb was cut away until it was bordered by the young larvae, and was then suspended in a box. Bees were shaken into the box, fed, and left confined for several days. In doing this, Jansha used the method later advocated by Dr. Miller and the "swarm box" that is still an integral part of many contemporary commercial queen rearing operations.

Development of Queen Rearing as a Commercial Beekeeping Activity

By the middle of the 1800's the basic knowledge of how to rear queen bees was available to beekeepers. Books, or sections of books, about honey bees had been published in Europe for centuries, and magazines devoted to bee culture were being published there. The lack of communication among beekeepers in the new world, however, impeded advancement. The appearance of the *American Bee Journal* in January 1861 and *Gleanings in Bee Culture* in January 1873 provided the channels through which beekeepers could become acquainted with all aspects of beekeeping. The journals also provided a forum for continuing dialogue among beekeepers, who then, as now, tended to be inventive, and they debated their ideas in letters to the journal, which were published, often with comments by the editor.

Queen rearing received comparatively little attention until after the importation of the Italian bee in 1861. The Italian possessed characteristics so superior to those of the black bees, that were reported to be in Virginia as early as 1622, that a demand for these bees grew rapidly. The importation of queens was rather difficult and many did not survive the overseas journey. Consequently, beekeepers who had imported Italian queens found there was a profitable market for queens, and queen rearing as a specialized beekeeping activity came into being.

Rearing Virgin Queens

Probably the first commercial queen rearer in the United States was L. L. Langstroth, who had received an Italian queen from C. J. Robinson in 1863. After the invention of his movable frame hive in 1851, Langstroth made use of the flexibility of his hive to secure queen cells. He reported in 1853 that in 1852 he removed the queen from a hive, inducing the bees to build queen cells. A week later he removed the queen from a second hive. The cells in the first hive were removed prior to emergence of the queens, and the queen from a third colony was transferred into the first hive. Later the cells of the second colony were similarly removed and the queen transferred from the first to the second colony. This rotation of the queen continued as long as cells were desired and probably represents the first queen rearing system.

During the next four decades several advances that were to be incorporated in queen rearing systems were made by beekeepers. Various ideas were tested, and only in the preparation of larvae for the cell building colonies was divergence in method substantial.

Obtaining and preparing larvae for cell builders. The earliest departure from merely letting queenless colonies produce queen cells from larvae in unmodified worker comb was probably that of Jansha 1771 (Alfonsus 1931), who cut away a newly built comb until the edge was bordered by "hardly noticeable larvae." In Langstroth's time, Obed (1861), after depriving a colony of its queen, made a horizontal cut in a comb containing eggs and young larvae. The bottom part of the comb was removed and the comb was reinserted into the queenless hive. Queen cells were constructed along the freshly cut margin of the comb that was left in the frame.

A. I. Root took this method a little farther by removing several horizontal strips from a comb, leaving a corresponding number of freshly cut comb margins with eggs and young larvae. This was later modified by Dr. Miller in his use of vertical strips of foundation fastened to the top bar of an empty frame which was placed in a hive with a breeder queen, and after comb was drawn and filled with eggs and young larvae it was transferred to a queenless cell builder.

In all of these variations the bees modified horizontal worker cells into vertical queen cells. In 1880, O. H. Townsend made the prepared cells open downward, as all prepared cells do in current queen rearing methods. He gave a selected queen a clean white worker comb. Four days later the comb with eggs and hatching larvae was cut into strips about ½ inch wide and as long as was convenient to handle. Each strip was fastened with pins to the side of an empty comb, near the top bar, and with the cells opening downward. The queen and two frames of brood and bees were removed from a strong colony. After the bees were shaken from the remaining combs, the combs were placed on other colonies, and the combs with prepared cells were put into the now queenless and broodless colony. J. M. Brooks (1880) improved on this by fastening the strips, after they were trimmed to within ¼ inch of the midrib, to the underside of the top bar of an empty frame and to two wooden bars, which he called "cell bars," that would fit between the end bars of the frame. In this way three strips with cells opening downward could be fastened within one frame.

Henry Alley (1882) employed the strip method in his commercial queen rearing. He kept his breeder queens in hives with five small frames, much like present day small frame nuclei, which he also used as hives for mating queens. Each day he gave each breeder colony a comb that had been newly drawn in other small hives. The combs were put into the breeder colony late in the day and left for 24 hours when they were transferred to other small hives for incubation. On the fourth day, the combs were cut into strips and attached with beeswax and rosin to the lower cut edge of other combs and put into cell builders. Alley's method of obtaining very young and lavishly fed larvae for queen rearing has not been surpassed, though Pritchard (1932a) made it more suitable for commercial queen rearing with his breeder queen hive-insert. Other satisfactory methods of restricting the queen to a limited comb area have been devised by beekeepers but all are based on the same principle.

Concurrently with Alley's development of his system of queen rearing other beekeepers were devising methods of their own. Their methods differed from Alley's largely by how larvae were prepared for the cell builder colonies. Huber in the late 1700's removed larvae from newly started queen cells and substituted young larvae from worker cells, thereby not only making the first larval transposition but also the first double graft. It was about one hundred years later in 1874 that this was repeated, this time by John L. Davis. He called the transfer of larvae his transposition process. Two years later in 1876, E. C. Larch performed the same operation and called it "grafting," a term that has persisted for any transfer of larvae from worker cells to queen cells or queen cell cups.

Apparently the first person to transfer larvae to queen cell cups rather than to newly started queen cells was W. L. Boyd (1878), who cut the natural cell cups or "acorns," or "embryo" cells as Doolittle called them, from combs and attached them to cell bars. He preceeded Brooks in the use of cell bars and also in positioning the prepared cells so they open downward. A. I. Root suggested dipping a wet stick into melted wax to form artificial queen cell cups, but this idea apparently lay unappreciated until Doolittle made it part of his queen rearing system.

Building the cells. Queenless colonies were the first to be used for building queen cells that were produced under the management of the beekeeper, and they continue to be used. The cells are usually started in such colonies and remain there until a day or two before emergence. These colonies are maintained by frequent addition of bees from other colonies or of sealed and emerging brood. Langstroth rotated queens between colonies and reared queens in the one temporarily without a queen.

Henry Alley (1883) started the cells with the aid of what he called a "swarming box" that was screened top and bottom and stocked with bees from a colony. The stocked box was set in a cool dark place for ten to twelve hours and was fed 50:50 sugar syrup from a mason jar with perforated lid that was set in a hole in the swarming box cover. Toward evening the bees from the swarming box were allowed to run through the entrance and into an empty cell building hive that was placed on the original stand in the apiary. The feeder was transferred from the swarming box to the broodless and queenless colony and the prepared strips were given. After the cells were sealed they were either given to mating nuclei or were caged in Alley's nursery cages and put into a queenless or queenright queen nursery.

Jansha had used the swarm box principle, and also new comb cut away to very young larvae, more than one hundred years earlier. He shook bees onto a prepared comb in a cage, fed the bees, and left the cells for several days for completion.

Alley's cell building system represented a great advance in control of cell building by the beekeeper. Starting the cells in a queenless, broodless colony, and finishing in other colonies has remained popular among queen rearers. Contemporary queen rearers may start cells in a confined queenless and broodless "swarm box" or other starting colony, or in a free flying queenless four or five frame hive that is maintained with sealed and emerging brood or with bees shaken from other colonies.

It became apparent in the 1880's that the transfer of young larvae from worker comb to queen cell cups had some distinct advantages over the cutting of combs with larvae into strips. Doolittle tested the various suggestions for queen rearing that came to his attention, and from the more practical ones and his own innovations he synthesized the queen rearing system used today (with only minor changes) by nearly all queen rearers.

Doolittle first tried raising queen cells in small nuclei that had three 5" x 6" frames, as was popular at the time. The resulting queens were disappointing. He next tried dequeening a colony during a flow of nectar and pollen and permitted the bees to build cells. Some of the queens that were produced looked to be fully developed queens and they performed well. However, in the spring one-third of his queens died so suddenly that no efforts had been made by the bees to supersede them. Seemingly, these queens had failed to attain the full development as queens that would extend their life span far beyond that of workers, and they died of "natural causes."

Other methods of cell raising were tried by Doolittle. Of these, only the harvest of swarm or supersedure cells, or double grafting into natural cells just started in colonies preparing to swarm pleased him, but the number of queens that could be produced by such means was severely limited, and demands for his queens prompted him to devise a method suitable for production of excellent virgins on a larger scale. In producing his cells, Doolittle in his first efforts dequeened a populous colony and fed it sugar syrup by means of a "division board" feeder he devised. He had noticed that colonies that had just been dequeened would not immediately start queen cells from larvae in the hive nor would they accept grafted queen cells that were "dry" grafted, but that three days after dequeening there would be developing cells. So the colony was fed for three days following removal of the queen before they were given cells to build. The colony was prepared three days after dequeening by removing all brood, leaving the other combs and a space for the frame with grafted cells. The cell cups were the natural cups found on combs and were fastened to the cut edge of a comb from which part had been removed, as Alley had done with his strips. The cells, which were dry when larvae were transferred into them, were left until the tenth day following grafting. As more cells were needed, this procedure was repeated with the colony which had received the brood from the first one. The queen and three frames of brood and bees were transferred to the first cell builder taking care that the queen was on the center comb when she was put into the first cell builder. The second cell builder was then prepared for cells. Doolittle also used a queenless cell nursery colony which was maintained by addition of sealed brood.

When dry grafted cells, such as were given to queenless colonies, were put into a colony that was preparing to swarm, the larvae were removed by the bees and the queen laid eggs in the cups, but newly started cells of swarming colonies that had been double grafted and left in the colony were highly successful. When such colonies were given grafted larvae in embryo cups that were supplied with a drop of royal jelly, acceptance was excellent. The placing of a drop of royal jelly into cell cups prior to transfer of the larvae is now known as "priming."

The supply of embryo cups was limited, and in obtaining them the combs upon which they were located were frequently damaged. Recalling Root's suggestion made in 1874 that artificial cups could be dipped, Doolittle modified a wooden rake tooth to fit accurately inside a natural queen cell cup, and using it he dipped cups from barely melted wax. These he attached with melted wax to cell bars after the manner of Brooks. The bar was inserted in the middle of a comb that had been prepared by removing a wide middle horizontal strip. Doolittle prepared the cells and grafted in a warm room, rather than in the apiary as was the practice when larvae were substituted for larvae in newly started swarm cells. He dated the top bars of the cell frames and kept a record in a notebook.

In a moment of curiosity, Doolittle gave a bar of grafted cells to a colony that was superseding its queen. The bees accepted eleven of twelve cells from which excellent queens emerged. Later, in 1883, acting on an idea he got from D. A. Jones, he found that bees built cells naturally when a queen was caged, and this led him to confine the queen of a colony to the lower body with a queen excluder and raise two combs of young larvae into the body above. A bar of grafted cells was put between the combs of larvae. The bees accepted the cells and lavishly supplied them with royal jelly. Subsequently, Doolittle gave the colony new cells as soon as the previous ones were sealed, leaving the sealed ones in the same hive. In some cases cells in nursery cages were left in the hive, and also caged virgins and even laying queens that were mated from nuclei that were constructed in the hive body with queen excluder material. He cautions that unsealed brood should be raised from below at least every ten days and to give no more than twelve grafted cells at one time. This is the modern starter-finisher cell builder, or the finisher when cells are started in starter colonies or swarm boxes.

In devising this method, Doolittle had assembled various contributions of others and his own innovations into a system of rearing virgin queens that is basically the system used by most queen rearers today.

Mating the Queens

Jansha (1771) was certainly one of the first to rear queens, and also one of the first to have them mated from small colonies. He introduced virgins of afterswarms to small colonies or distributed swarm cells to such colonies. In establishing the mating colonies, which may actually have been new ones for colony increase, he shook bees in abundance onto a comb, fed them well, and kept them confined for several days (Alphonsus 1931).

Langstroth employed all of the methods for obtaining laying queens of his time, including division of the brood and bees of a colony to form new colonies as Huber had done with his leaf hive. He emphasized the new colony should be restricted to one side of the hive body by means of a divider or movable partition, now known as a "follower" board, or sometimes as a "division" board. He also confined the new colonies for one to three days before opening the entrance, which was done about an hour before sunset. He called these new colonies "nuclei," a term that is now usually restricted to queen mating colonies. New colonies from established colonies that are made up for increase of colony numbers are now commonly called "divisions" or "divides." Langstroth devised another way of creating new colonies by dividing swarms into several parts and giving each division a cell or a virgin queen. Artificial swarms would serve also. The natural or artificial swarm was hived in a box, all openings of which were closed, and it was taken to a cool, dark cellar. About an hour before sunset, hives containing some combs were set out for the divisions of the swarm and each was given a queen cell, or a comb with young larvae. The swarm was then brought up from the cellar and the bees shaken out upon a sheet where they were sprinkled gently with sugar syrup. About a quart of bees was scooped up for each division and deposited on the hive entrance. By morning each division was firmly established.

This procedure, is in principle, practically the same as that followed in the formation of baby nuclei by commercial queen breeders, except the nuclei are always confined in a cool, dark place for about three days before they are set on location. When Langstroth wrote his book in 1853, queen rearing was entirely a matter of each beekeeper's providing his own queens. Nuclei that were used strictly for mating were unknown, but the term "nuclei" was gradually appropriated by commercial queen rearers to designate queen mating colonies. It is cause for wonder that Langstroth, and Dzierzon in Europe who developed procedures along parallel lines, worked out a method of making colony increase that would be so similar to that of establishing baby nuclei by commercial queen rearers.

Obed (1861) put cells or virgins in a small box furnished with maturing worker brood and a few hundred bees. In doing this, he utilized the method of mating queens from baby nuclei, which was later advocated by Root (Editorial 1878).

Langstroth adopted the German plan of confining a queen to be introduced to a colony in a queen cage, which was simply a hole bored part way through a block of wood and closed with screen wire. After about 24 hours she was released, though virgin queens were more likely than laying queens to be killed by the bees. By providing another hole large enough for the queen to pass through, and closing it with wax, the bees would release the queen themselves. Langstroth also constructed nursery cages for surplus cells by making a frame of solid board and boring holes through it which he closed on both sides with slides of excluder. The nursery frame with its cells or virgins was kept in a queenless nursery colony.

In 1873 E. Gerry reported that he divided a hive body into three compartments, each with an entrance on a side different from the others. In these he established small colonies and gave each a queen cell. These were modern standard frame mating nuclei, but Gerry used them to overwinter surplus queens.

Though Langstroth may have been the first American commercial queen breeder, Henry Alley was probably the first one to rear and sell queens on a large scale. He gave us the swarm box for starting cells, a simple nursery cage that remains the standard one, and extensive use of small nuclei for queen mating. Bees for establishment of nuclei were confined for ten to twelve hours in the swarming box after which they would accept virgins when they were installed in the mating boxes. After installation, the bees in the mating hives were confined for seventy-two hours by means of a ventilating screen attached to the entrance that permitted them to crawl on the front of the hive. Present day beekeepers use this screen as a moving screen, and the robber screen is simply an adaptation of this screen for colony protection. The nursery cages with surplus cells were put into either queenless or queenright colonies, and each was provided with candy as food for the virgins.

Doolittle commented that "there are nearly as many ways of forming nuclei as there are different individuals who make them," and he outlined four methods in use at the time. These are still used. Doolittle preferred standard frame nuclei to the smaller ones and when queen rearing was over for the year he combined the nuclei into full colonies for wintering. The method of forming nuclei he used most often was similar to that of Alley's. He made small screened "nucleus boxes" for each nucleus to be formed. Between 9 and 11 a.m., bees to form nuclei were set on combs outside their hives until they were filled with honey, when they were shaken from the combs through a funnel into the boxes. The boxes with bees were then taken to the cellar. About four hours after the boxes were stocked a virgin queen was released among the bees in each of them, and just before sunset the bees were installed in their nuclei by shaking them from the boxes into the hives. A frame of honey and a frame with sealed brood were given each, but no unsealed brood. The nuclei were individually housed in one side of standard bodies in a space limited by a division board against the frames.

Alley gave a "ripe" cell to a nucleus immediately after removing a laying queen. Doolittle encountered much loss of virgin queens when he gave a nucleus a queen cell immediately after a laying queen was removed. It occurred to him that since queen cells are always destroyed from the side, if the bees are denied access to the sides the cell would not be destroyed. To accomplish this he made a cone of screen wire to enclose the cell, except that an opening the size of a pencil was left at the apex of the cone to expose the lower end of the cell so the queen could emerge to join the bees in the colony. N. D. West (1906) some years later made and patented the West spiral cell protector that was based on the same principle. Doolittle fastened the ripe cells to the combs of nuclei by pressing the base of the cells into the comb, or, in hot weather, by fixing the cells between the top bars of adjacent frames. This is common practice today. He warned that queens in queen cells can be injured if the cells are shaken to dislodge bees from them; and in cool weather he transported ripe cells to nuclei in a box lined with felt and warmed with a scale weight heated to a temperature comfortable to the hands. He preferred to leave queen cells in the cell builder until a day or two before emergence and disliked the "lamp-nursery" that had been devised by F. R. Shaw in 1873 (Editorial 1878a). Nevertheless, the lamp-nursery was popular and was the forerunner of the incubator that is used by many present day queen rearers to hold queen cells for a day before they are put into nuclei.

Loss of queens on their mating flight was sometimes excessive. Buchanan (1881) pointed out that many queens are lost in trying to enter the wrong hive when returning from the mating flight and he suggested mating nuclei should be arranged for easier orientation by the queens and that landmarks be provided. Unfortunately losses from this cause still occur.

In 1883, A. A. Fradenburg accidentally had a virgin queen emerge in a honey super. He gave the super an entrance, and the queen flew and mated. When Doolittle learned of this, he experimented with mating virgin queens from honey supers in which an entrance was provided at the back. The success of this experiment encouraged Doolittle to modify a hive body for use as both a honey super and as two nuclei for mating virgin queens. He prepared several bodies so that a sheet of queen excluder could be slid down between the ends of the body three and one-half inches from either side. Each sheet of excluder formed, with the body sidewall, a compartment that could contain two frames. Each compartment had a hole cut into the back as an entrance. The bottom of both compartments was closed by an excluder between the modified super and the body below. Doolittle found it was necessary to have "dummy" frames below the compartments, or to cover the excluder below the compartments with screen so the queens in the compartments would be completely separated form the queen in the broodnest below them. A frame with some brood was placed in each compartment, along with a queen cell. The entrances were closed until the virgins were about six days old.

Other beekeepers later obtained mated queens from bodies which were stocked with brood and bees from the broodnest below, and which were placed over the broodnest above an "enameled" cloth, or above an inner cover, with an entrance to the rear of the hive. The modern "board divide" is essentially the same arrangement, and while it is an excellent way to have queens mated for use in a beekeeper's own apiary, it is not suitable for producing large numbers of queens for sale.

Shipping Queens

Until beekeepers became interested in Italian bees there was little demand for queens and thus little need to ship them.

The first Italian queens that arrived alive in the United States were imported in 1859, apparently in full colonies, by Samuel Wagner and Richard Colvin from Dzierzon's apiary. P. G. Mahan also imported some colonies the same year. Further importations of Italian colonies, this time from Italy, were made in 1860 by S. B. Parsons, and in 1861 by William G. Rose. In 1863 and 1864 Langstroth received queens from Dzierzon. In 1867 Adam Grimm imported "large" numbers of Italian queens from Italy, and this was followed in 1874 and later by numerous queens being imported by C. P. Dadant from Italy. A. I. Root and several others also imported Italian queens (Phillips 1920; Dadant 1927). Importation of Italian queens and queens of other races continued until 1923 when importations were prohibited as a measure to prevent the introduction of *Acarapis woodi* into the United States.

Soon after the first importations were made, Italian queens that were shipped across the ocean were confined in various kinds of cages with bees and combs with honey instead of in colonies. The honey frequently leaked, and successful shipments were few. C. P. Dadant after 1874 found that queens with about fifty to seventy-five attendant workers confined in a box about three inches deep, three inches wide, and four inches long with two small frames of comb, one with thick sugar syrup, and one dry, and with air holes in the sides made the thirty-six day journey with little loss (Dadant 1913).

In the United States queens were first shipped by express but because of the inconvenient location of express offices a better method of transportation was desirable. Apparently the first shipment by mail was made by C. J. Robinson to Langstroth in 1863. In 1868 Quinby shipped queens short distances by mail (Pellett 1939), and in the same year Alley and also J. H. Townley were credited with shipping queens by mail (Dadant 1927).

The first domestic queen cages were simply a block of wood about two inches square and one and one-half inches thick. A large hole bored to within one-fourth inch of the bottom, with the opening covered with screen wire, formed the container for the queen and her attendants. Food for the bees was honey in a piece of comb that had been cleaned by bees after it was cut which was fastened in place in the cage hole with a wooden pin (Pellett 1938).

The honey used as food for the caged bees often leaked in transit, and this, with the occasional sting suffered by mail clerks, prompted the postal service in 1872 to prohibit sending bees by mail (Alley 1873). Alley had used a sponge soaked in honey as a means of feeding the bees in transit, but after the postal ruling he changed to a sponge moistened with water and two or three lumps of loaf sugar. The prohibition against mailing queens caused dismay among beekeepers and a concerted effort was begun to have the ruling repealed. In 1880 those efforts, aided by help from Professor Cook, were successful in gaining a modification of the ruling so bees were permitted to be shipped by mail, provided honey was not used as food and the bees were screened in such a way they could not sting the mail handlers (Editorial 1880a, 1880b).

Beekeepers turned to candy as a substitute for honey as a shipping food. Pure sugar candy made by boiling sugar and water had been used in Germany by Mr. Weigel for feeding colonies for some time. The Reverend Scholz recommended a softer candy be fed instead of the hard sugar candy of Mr. Weigel. Scholz mixed heated honey and "pounded" lump sugar and worked it into a "stiff, doughy mass." This he cut into slices, or formed cakes or lumps, which he wrapped in coarse linen and placed in frames. This candy was not meant for shipping queens, but it was later used for this purpose with powdered sugar being substituted for the pounded sugar.

In the United States, I. R. Good (1881) prepared candy for shipping queens that was similar to the Scholz candy except that he made the candy with granulated sugar and unboiled honey. This was apparently relatively satisfactory, but since unboiled honey could spread American foulbrood, boiling was resorted to. When the sugar was mixed with hot honey the candy would harden in the queen cages and often the bees starved enroute. Phillips and Smith (Nolan 1924) recommended that cold invert sugar syrup be used in place of honey. Frank Benton pounded sugar to a fine powder and mixed it with honey in making candy for shipping queens from overseas to the United States; and Root used the finest pulverized confectioner's sugar (Good 1884). The combination of powdered sugar and invert syrup is the basis for present day queen cage candy and is known as Good candy.

The shipping cage used by contemporary queen rearers was devised by Frank Benton about 1883 (Pellett 1938) for the purpose of shipping queens of various races from overseas to the United States. In Benton's cage there were three connecting compartments in a rectangular block of wood with a smaller hole at each end extending from the cage end to the nearer compartment. One of the compartments was filled with candy, and the queen and workers occupied the other two. The cage was closed with a strip of screen wire over the top and corks in the end holes. This cage resembled the Peet cage that had been popular as a shipping and introducing cage.

The slightly modified Benton cage, provisioned with a Scholz-Good type candy, has been an extremely successful instrument to ship queens by mail. It is not perfect but is reasonably satisfactory. Fryer in 1861 maintained that bees need water, and Woodrow (1941) showed queens need water for survival and bees need water to utilize candy over a protracted period. Root (1878) attempted to provide water to queens in transit but was unable to design a suitable device for this. The inclusion of a small proportion of glycerine in the candy, as was used by Manum in 1889, tends to keep candy soft.

In Retrospect

When we consider the heritage left us by those who have gone before, we gladly agree with Sir Isaac Newton that "If I have seen farther than others, it is because I have stood on the shoulders of giants," and with Henry Malcolm Fraser (1931) that "In short, these pages show how, in almost every respect, the modern beekeeper is the child and descendant of the old."

REFERENCES

Achord, W. D., 1932. Package business 20 years old. Glean. Bee Cult. **60**(5): 294-295.

Adam, A., 1913. Bau und Mechanismus des Receptaculum seminis bei den Bienen, Wespen, und Ameisen. Zool. Jahrb. Anat. **35**:1-74.

Alfonsus, Erwin C., 1931. The life of Anton Jansha. Amer. Bee Jour. **71**(11): 508-509.

Alley, H., 1873. Sending queens by mail. Amer. Bee Jour. **9**(5):109-110.

Alley, H., 1881. Friend Alley on queen-cages. Glean. Bee Cult. **9**(6):269.

Alley, Henry, 1882. The Bee-Keeper's Handy Book. Publ. by author. Salem Press, Salem, Mass.

Alley, Henry, 1883. The Bee-Keeper's Handy Book. Publ. by author. Wenham, Mass.

Ambroise, Victor, 1924. Report on the selection of bees and choice of males for impregnation. From: VIIth International Congress of Bee-Keepers, Quebec, Sept. 1-4, 1924.

Atwater, E. F., 1906. A nursery and introducing-cage combined. Glean. Bee Cult. **34**(15):1070.

Atwater, E. F. and J. E. Thompson, 1919. Cages with Chantry feature. Glean. Bee Cult. 42(8):496-498.

Aristotle (384-322 BC), On the Generation of Animals. Book 3, Chapter 10. In: Great Books of the Western World, 9:300-302, Encyclopedia Britannica, Inc., Chicago.

Aristotle (384-322 BC), History of Animals. Book 5, Chapters 21 and 23. In: Great Books of the Western World 9:80-88, 131, 149-153. Encyclopedia Britannica, Inc., Chicago.

Beetsma, J., 1979. The process of queen-worker differentiation in the honeybee. Bee World 60(1):24-29.

Berlepsch, The Baron of 1861. The Dzierzon theory. Amer. Bee Jour. 1:1-10, 25-27, 49-51, 73-76, 97-99, 121-125, 145-148, 169-172, 199-202, 223-226. Transl. by Samuel Wagner of Berlepsch's "Apistical Letters."

Berlepsch, August Baron von, 1869. Die Biene und ihre zucht mit beweglichen. Waben. 2nd edition. J. Schneider, Mannheim.

Bertholf, L. M., 1925. The moults of the honeybee. Jour. Econ. Ent. 18(2): 380-384.

Beven, Edward, 1838. The Honey-Bee. Baldwin, Cradock Jay, London.

Bichtler, Ernst, 1960. Im Bienenland. Deutscher Landwirtschaftsverlag, Berlin.

Bishop, G. H., 1920. Fertilization in the honey-bee. I. The male sexual organs: their histological structure and physiological functioning. II. Disposal of the sexual fluids in the organs of the female. Jour. Expt. Zool. 31(2): 225-265, 267-286.

Blochmann, F., 1889. Uber die Zahl der Richtungskorper bei befruchteten und unbefruchteten Bieneneiern. Morph. Jahrb. 15:85-96.

Boyd, W. L., 1878. Queen cells to order. Glean. Bee Cult. 6(10):323.

Brooks, Jas. M., 1880. How to get plenty of choice queen cells. Another way. Glean. Bee Cult. 8(8):362.

Bruennich, Dr., 1913. Fertilizing queens at a mating station. Glean. Bee Cult. 41(14):493-497.

Buchanan, J. A., 1881. Queen-rearing. Queens getting lost on their wedding trip; cause and remedy. Glean. Bee Cult. 9(9):445.

Butler, Charles, 1609. The Feminine Monarchy, or the History of Bees.

Camargo, C. A. de, 1972. Aspectos da reproducao dos Apideos sociais. Dissertacao apresentada a Faculdade de Medicina de Ribeirao Preto, (USPP) para obtencao do Grau de Mestre em Ciencias.

Camargo, J. M. F. de, and L. S. Goncalves, 1971. Manipulation procedures in the technique of instrumental insemination of the queen honeybee (A.m.L.). Apidologie 2:239-246.

Camargo, J. M. F., and M. L. S. Mello, 1970. Anatomy and histology of the genital tract, spermatheca, spermathecal duct and glands of *Apis mellifera* queens (Hymenoptera: Apidae). Apidologie 1(4):351-373.

Chambers, Lee, 1880. Marking the queen. Glean. Bee Cult. 8(4):175.

Cheshire, F., 1886. Bees and Beekeeping. Vol. I; 1888 Vol. II. London.

Dadant, Ch., 1874. On the size of the frame. Glean. Bee Cult. 2(3):29.

Dadant, C. P., 1873. Improvements in bee culture. Glean. Bee Cult. 1(9):67.

Dadant, C. P., 1913. Langstroth on the Hive and Honey Bee. Dadant and Sons, Hamilton, Illinois.

Dadant, C. P., 1927. Langstroth on the Hive and Honey Bee. The American Bee Journal, Hamilton, Illinois.

Dadant, M. G., 1946. The production of queens and package bees. In: The Hive and the Honey Bee, Roy A. Grout, editor. pp. 555-569. Dadant and Sons, Hamilton, Illinois.

Davis, John L., 1874. (under: Heads of Grain from Different Fields). Glean. Bee Cult. 2(9):107.

Dietz, A., 1970 (1966). The influence of environmental and nutritional factors on growth and caste determination of female honey bees. Apic. Abst.: 887/70. Abstract of Ph.D. Dissertation. Univ. of Minnesota, 1966.

Doolittle, G. M., 1880. Introducing queens. Glean. Bee Cult. 8(4):158-159.

Doolittle, G. M., 1881. How to rear good queens. Glean. Bee Cult. 9(8):375-376.

Doolittle, G. M., 1888. Scientific Queen-Rearing. 6th Edition. American Bee Journal, Hamilton, Illinois.

Doolittle, G. M., 1899. Queen-cells above perforated honey-boards. Glean. Bee Cult. 17(13):532-534.

Doull, K. M., 1974. Effect of distance on the attraction of pollen to honeybees in the hive. Jour. Apic. Res. 13(1):27-32.

DuPraw, E. J., 1961. A unique hatching process in the honeybee. Trans. Amer. Micr. Soc. 80(2):185-191.

Dzierzon, 1861. Development of the queen. Amer. Bee Jour. 1(12):265-266.

Eckert, J. E., 1934. Studies in the number of ovarioles in queen honey-bees in relation to body size. Jour. Econ. Ent. 27(3):629-635.

Eckert, John E., and Frank R. Shaw, 1960. Beekeeping. The Macmillan Company, New York.

Editorial, 1861a. The Dzierzon theory. Amer. Bee Jour. 1(1):5-6.

Editorial, 1861b. Copulation of the queen bee. Amer. Bee Jour. 1(3):65-66.

Editorial, 1861c. Vitality of spermatazoa. Amer. Bee Jour. 1(9):213.

Editorial, 1878a. Lamp nursery. Glean. Bee Cult. 6(9):295-296.

Editorial, 1878b. Nucleus. Glean. Bee Cult. 6(9):298-300.

Editorial, 1880a. Good news! Good news for all! Prof. Cook has succeeded, and queens can once more go by mail. Glean. Bee Cult. 8(2):65.

Editorial, 1880b. Cages for queens to go by mail. Glean. Bee Cult. 8(3):106-108.

Editorial, 1881. The new industry; work for beekeepers. The great call for bees by the pound. Glean. Bee Cult. 9(6):274-275.

Editorial, 1913. Water for bees in mailing cages and for shipment by express; a big stride in advance. Glean. Bee Cult. 41:595-596.

Flanagan, E. I., 1881. Friend Flanagan's first experience in selling bees by the pound. Glean. Bee Cult. 9(6):269-270.

Flanders, S. E., 1977. The tracheal envelope of the queen's spermatheca. Bee World 58(4):150-152.

Fooshe, J. D., 1889. Rearing cells in strong colonies containing a laying queen. Glean. Bee Cult. 17(12):489-490.

Fooshe, J. D., 1893. Queen-cells from drone comb. Glean. Bee Cult. 21(15):635.

Foti, N., 1973. Data on the control of migration of spermatozoa in queens (*Apis mellifica* L.). In: Proceedings of the 24th International Apicultural Congress, Buenos Aires, Argentina, pp. 345-347.

Fradenburg, A. A., 1883. How to get queen-cells with the old queen in the hive. Glean. Bee Cult. 11(1):12-13.

Fraser, Henry Malcolm, 1931. Beekeeping in Antiquity. Univ. of London Press, Ltd. London.

Fryer, J., 1861. Bees: water essential to their prosperity. Amer. Bee Jour. 1(4):80.

Gallup, E., 1880. Gallup. Some of his ideas in regard to queen rearing and improving bees generally. Glean. Bee Cult. 8(5):213.

Garófalo, Carlos Alberto, 1977. Broad viability in normal colonies of *Apis mellifera*. Jour. Apic. Res. 16(1):3-13.

Gerry, E., 1873. Surplus queens. Amer. Bee Jour. 9(1):8-9.

Good, I. R., 1881. Holy-land bees; candy for queen-cages, etc. Glean. Bee Cult. 9(8):374.

Good, I. R., 1884. Benton's wonderful success in mailing queens all over the world. Glean. Bee Cult. 12(21):728-729.

Gravenhorst, 1868. To prevent or arrest robbing. Amer. Bee Jour. 4(4):61. (from Bienenzeitung)

Hardesty, Geo., 1867. Introducing queens. Amer. Bee Jour. 3(3):49.

Harp, Emmett R., 1973. A specialized system for multiple rearing of quality honeybee queens. Amer. Bee Jour. 113(7):256-258, 261.

Haydak, Mykola H., 1943. Larval food and development of castes in the honeybee. Jour. Econ. Ent. 36(5):778-792.

Haydak, M. H., and A. E. Vivino, 1950. The changes in the thiamin, riboflavin, niacin, and pantothenic acid content in the food of female honeybees during growth with a note on the vitamin activity of royal jelly and bee bread. Ann. Ent. Soc. Amer. 43:361-367.

Heberle, J. A., 1913. Mating stations. Glean. Bee Cult. 41(14):497-498.

Heddon, James, 1885. Success in Bee-Culture. Times Print, Dowagiac, Michigan.

Huber, Francis, 1814. New Observations Upon Bees. Transl. by C. P. Dadant (1926). American Bee Journal, Hamilton, Illinois.

Hughes, J. S., 1884. Drones and queens. Positive proof that drones do collect in bodies in swarming-time. Glean. Bee Cult. 12(5):160.

Hutchinson, W. Z., 1880. Notes from the Banner Apiary. No. 5. Raising queens and extracted honey. Glean. Bee Cult. 8(4):151-152.

Hutchinson, W. Z., 1891. Advanced Bee-Culture. The Review Print (Beekeepers Review). Flint, Mich.

Hutchinson, W. Z., 1905. Advanced Bee Culture. The Review Print (Beekeepers Review). Flint, Mich.

Janscha, A., 1771. Abhandlung von Schwärmen der Bienen. Wein. Summarized in Anton Janscha on the swarming of bees. Transl. by H. M. Fraser (1951). Royston, Herts, Apis Club.

Jay, S. Cameron, 1962. Colour changes in honeybee pupae. Bee World 43(4): 119-122.

Jay, S. Cameron, 1963. The development of honeybees in their cells. Jour. Apic. Res. 2:117-134.

Jaycox, E. R., 1961. The effects of various foods and temperatures on sexual maturity of drone honeybee (Apis mellifera). Ann. Ent. Soc. Amer., 54(4): 519-523.

Johansson, T. S. K., and M. P. Johansson, 1973. Methods for rearing queens. Bee World 54(4):149-175.

Kelmore, 1903. Painting queens. Bees 4(2):37-38.

Kerr, Warwick Estevam, 1973. New approaches in the genetics and cytogenetics of bees. In: Proc. VII Congr. IUSSI, London, pp. 182-192.

Kerr, Warwick E., and Harry H. Laidlaw, Jr., 1956. General genetics of bees. Advances in Genetics, VIII: 109-153.

Kinard, W. P., 1947. Hints on installing spring packages. Southern Beekeeper 1(3):14-15.

Koeniger, N., 1970. Factors determining the laying of drone and worker eggs by the queen honeybee. Bee World 51(4):166-169.

Laidlaw, Harry H., Jr., 1944. Artificial insemination of the queen bee (Apis mellifera L.): Morphological basis and results. Jour. Morph. 74(3):429-465.

Laidlaw, Harry H., Jr., 1949. Development of precision instruments for artificial insemination of queen bees. Jour. Econ. Ent. 42(2):254-261.

Laidlaw, H. H., 1954. Beekeeping management for the bee breeder. Amer. Bee Jour. 94:92-95.

Laidlaw, Harry H., Jr., 1958. Organization and operation of a bee breeding program. Tenth International Congress of Entomology Proceedings (1956) 4:1067-1078.

Laidlaw, H. H., 1974. Relationships of bees within a colony. Apiacta 9(2):49-52.

Laidlaw, H. H., 1975. Queen Rearing. Amer. Bee Jour. 115(10):384-387.

Laidlaw, Harry H., Jr., 1977. Instrumental Insemination of Honey Bee Queens. Dadant and Sons, Inc., Hamilton, Illinois.

Laidlaw, Harry H., Jr. and J. E. Eckert, 1962. Queen Rearing. University of California Press, Berkeley. 2nd ed.

Langstroth, L. L., 1853. Langstroth on the Hive and the Honey-Bee. A. I. Root Co., Medina, Ohio.

Langstroth, L. L., 1861. To introduce an Italian queen in a colony of common bees. Amer. Bee Jour. 1(5):100.

Larch, E. C. L., M.D., 1876. Grafting queen cells. Glean. Bee Cult. 4(3):48.

Leuckart, Professor (of Giessen), 1861. The sexuality of bees. Amer. Bee Jour. 1(11):241-250.

Mackensen, Otto, 1943. The occurrence of parthenogenetic females in some strains of honey bees. Jour. Econ. Ent. 36(3):465-467.

Mackensen, Otto, 1947. Effect of carbon dioxide on initial oviposition of artificially inseminated and virgin queens. Jour. Econ. Ent. 40(3):344-349.

Mackensen, O., 1951. Viability and sex determination in the honey bee (*Apis mellifera* L.). Genetics 36(5):500-509.

Mackensen, Otto, 1955. Experiments in the technique of artificial insemination of queen bees. Jour. Econ. Ent. 48(4):418-421.

Mackensen, O., 1964. Relation of semen volume to success in artificial insemination of queen honey bees. Jour. Econ. Ent. 57(4):581-583.

Mackensen, Otto, and W. C. Roberts, 1948. A manual for the artificial insemination of queen bees. U.S.D.A. Bur. Ent. and Pl. Quar. ET-250.

Mackensen, Otto, and Kenneth W. Tucker, 1970. Instrumental insemination of queen bees. USDA Agricultural Handbook No. 390, Washington, D. C.

McLain, Nelson W., 1887. The control of reproduction. Report of experiments in apiculture. In: Report U.S. Comm. Agric. 1886:589-591.

Manum, A. E., 1889. Manum in the apiary with his men. Glean. Bee Cult. 17(15):628-629.

Martin, J. H., 1874. Pollen. Its relation to brood-rearing. Glean. Bee Cult. 2(10):116.

Melampy, R. M., and D. Breese Jones, 1939. Chemical composition and vitamin content of royal jelly. In: Proc. Soc. Exp. Biol. and Med. 41:382-388.

Merrill, S. E., 1932. Better packaging and better handling in transit have almost eliminated losses. Glean. Bee Cult. 60(3):154.

Miller, C. C., 1912. How best queen cells can be secured. Amer. Bee Jour. 52(8):243.

Muenzberg, Joseph, 1775. Des Anton Jansha sel. sehr erfahrenen Bienenwirthes und Kaiserl. Lehrers der Bienenzucht zu Wien hinterlassenen Vollstaendige Lehre von Bienenzucht Vienna.

Murry, H. D., 1921. Classifying the queens. Glean. Bee Cult. 49(6):347-348.

Nelson, James Allen, 1915. The Embryology of the Honey Bee. Princeton University Press, Princeton.

Nelson, James A., Arnold P. Sturtevant, and Bruce Lineburg, 1924. Growth and feeding of honeybee larvae. USDA Dept. Bulletin No. 1222.

Nolan, W. J., 1924a. Localization of queen-rearing. Glean. Bee Cult. 52(12):760-765.

Nolan, W. J., 1924b. Development of queen-rearing in the United States. VIIth International Congress of Bee-Keepers. Quebec, Sept. 1-4, 1924. pp. 298-310.

Nolan, W. J., 1932. Breeding the honeybee under controlled conditions. USDA Tech. Bul. 326.

Nolan, W. J., 1937. Improved apparatus for inseminating queen bees by the Watson method. Jour. Econ. Ent. 30:700-705.

Obed, 1861. Raising queens. Amer. Bee Jour. 1(6):143.

Oertel, E., 1930. Metamorphosis of the honeybee. Jour. Morph. and Physiol. 50:295-340.

Oertel, E., 1940. Mating flights of queen bees. Glean. in Bee Cult. 68(5):292-3, 333.

Onions, G. W., 1912. South African "fertile-worker" bees. Agric. Jour. Union S. Africa, 3:720.

Park, O. W., 1949. The honey-bee colony — life history. In: The Hive and the Honey Bee. Edited by Roy A. Grout. Dadant and Sons, Hamilton, Illinois.

Pellett, Frank Chapman, 1938. History of American Beekeeping. Collegiate Press, Inc., Ames, Iowa.

Peschetz, Hans, 1947. Der Weg zur besten Honigbiene. Ploetz und Theiss, Wolfsberg, Kännten, Osterreich.

Phillips, Everett Franklin, 1928. Beekeeping. The MacMillan Co., N.Y.

Phillips, Geo. W., 1903. Modern queen-rearing. Glean. Bee Cult. 31(24):1048-1050.

Phin, John, 1884. A Dictionary of Practical Apiculture. The Industrial Publication Company, N.Y.

Planta, Dr. A. von, 1888. Ueber den Futtersaft der Bienen. Zeitschr. f. phys. chemie von Hoppe-Seyler. XII(4):327-354; XIII(6):552-561. Also in Schweizerische Bienen-zeitung (1888), 11(8 and 9):237-255.

Planta, Dr. A. von, 1889. Nochmals über den Futtersaft der Bienen. Schweizerische Bienen-Zeitung. 12(10):293-298.

Polhemus, M. S., J. L. Lush, and W. C. Rothenbuhler, 1950. Mating systems in honeybees. Jour. Hered. 41:151-155.

Posel, 1784. (A Complete Treatise of Forest and Horticulture Bee-Culture). (Cited by Langstroth 1903.) Munich.

Pridgen, W. H., 1900. Commercial queen-rearing in all of its details. Amer. Bee Jour. 40(26):401-405.

Pritchard, Mel, 1932a. Selecting best larvae for queen rearing. Glean. Bee Cult. 60(2):76-78.

Pritchard, Mel, 1932b. Queen cells by the thousand. Glean. Bee Cult. 60(3): 147-150.

Pritchard, Mel, 1932c. From cell builders to nuclei. Glean. Bee Cult. 60(4): 216-218.

Pritchard, Mel, 1932d. Baby nuclei for mating queens. Glean. Bee Cult. 60(5): 280-281.

Quinby, M., 1873. Bees by mail. Amer. Bee Jour. 9(2):37.

Reaumur, R. A. F., 1740. Memoires Pour Servir a l'Histoire des Insects. 6 vols. De l'Imprimerie Royal, Paris. (Cited in Huber 1814.)

Ribbands, C. R., 1953. The Behaviour and Social Life of Honeybees. Bee Research Association Limited, London.

Roberts, W. C., 1944. Multiple mating of queen bees proved by progeny and flight tests. Glean. Bee Cult. 72(6):255-259, 303.

Roberts, William C., 1947. A syringe for artificial insemination of honeybees. Jour. of Econ. Ent. 40(3):445-446.

Roberts, William C. and Otto Mackensen, 1951. Breeding improved honey bees. Amer. Bee Jour. 91(7):292-294; (8):328-330; (9):382-384; (10):418-421; (11):473-475.

Roberts, William C., and Ward Stanger, 1969. Survey of the package bee and queen industry. Amer. Bee Jour. 109(1):8-11.

Root, A. I., 1874. Answer to problems, etc. Answer to problem No. 23. Glean. Bee Cult. 2(8):89.

Root, A. I., 1878. How to keep extra queens almost any length of time. Glean. Bee Cult. 6:288-290.

Root, A. I., 1880. Our own apiary, honey farm, and factory. Bees by the pound. Glean. Bee Cult. 8(8):368.

Root, E. R., 1900 (Editorial). The various modern methods of queen-rearing compared. Glean. Bee Cult. 28(17):694-695.

Rosenthal, Cora, 1969. Relatiile intre indivizii familiei de albine. Apicultura 22(10):4-8.

Rothenbuhler, W. C., 1957. Diploid male tissue as new evidence on sex determination in honey bees. Jour. Hered. 48(4):160-168.

Rothenbuhler, W. C., 1958. Genetics and breeding of the honey bee. Ann. Rev. Ent. 3:161-180.

Rothenbuhler, Walter C., Jovan M. Kulincevic, and Warwick E. Kerr, 1968. Bee Genetics. In: Ann. Rev. Genetics 2:413-438.

Ruttner, Friedrich, 1957. Die sexualfunktionon der honigbienen in dienst ihrer sozialen gemeinschaft. Zeitschrift für vergleichende Physiologie. Bd 39:577-600.

Ruttner, Friedrich, 1964. Zur technik und anwendung der knustlichen besamung der bienenkönigen. Zeitschrift für Bienenforschung. 7(2):25-34, April.

Ruttner, Friedrich, ed., 1976. The Instrumental Insemination of the Queen Bee. Apimondia International Beekeeping Technology and Economy Institute. Bucharest, Romania.

Ruttner, F. and G. Koeniger, 1971. Die Füllung der Spermatheka der Bienenkönigin. Ztschr. f. Vergl. Physiol. 72:411-422.

Ruttner, F., and Otto Mackensen, 1952. The genetics of the honeybee. Bee World 33(4):53-62; (5):71-79.

Schirach, A. G., 1771. Historie Naturelle de la Reine des Abeilles, avec l'Art de Former des Essaims. The Hague (cited in Huber 1814).

Shafer, Geo. D., 1917. A study of the factors which govern mating in the honey bee. Mich. Ag. Col. Exp. Sta. Tech. Bul. 34.

Shuel, R. W., S. E. Dixon, and G. B. Kinoshita, 1978. Growth and development of honeybees in the laboratory on altered queen and worker diets. Jour. Apic. Res. 17(2):57-68.

Siebold, Prof. C.T.E. von, 1867a. On the reproduction of bees. Amer. Bee Jour. 3(4):73-75.

Siebold, Prof. C.T.E. von, 1867b. True parthenogenesis in the honey bee. Amer. Bee Jour. 3(5):81-86 and subsequent issues.

Simpson, J., 1954. Effect of some anesthetics on honeybees. Bee World 35:149-155.

Smith, Jay, 1919. Safe introduction of queens — not the average fifty per cent loss in introduction. Glean. Bee Cult. 42(8):498-500.

Smith, Jay, 1923. Queen Rearing Simplified. A. I. Root Co., Medina, Ohio.

Smith, Jay, 1933. Rearing your own queens. Amer. Bee Jour. 73(3):93-94.

Smith, Jay, 1947. Queens direct from the egg. Southern Beekeeper 1(3):6-10.

Smith, Jay, 1949. Better Queens. Published by the author.

Snelgrove, L. E., 1949. Queen Rearing. Publ. by Miss I. Snelgrove, Bleadon, Somerset, England.

Snodgrass, R. E., 1956. Anatomy of the Honey Bee. Comstock Publishing Associates, Cornell University Press, Ithaca, N.Y.

Standefer, W. F., 1874. Early queens from the south. Glean. Bee Cult. 2(5):56.

Stehle, R., 1881. Candy for queen cages. Glean. Bee Cult. 9(9):434.

Swarthmore (E. L. Pratt), 1900. Queens by the peck. Swarthmore's new queen-cell hatchery; a new and simple method of making queen-cups; how to keep a plurality of queens in one hive over winter. Glean. Bee Cult. 28(23):917-918.

Swarthmore (E. L. Pratt), 1901. The Swarthmore system of queen-rearing. Glean. Bee Cult. 29(10):434-437; (12):504-507; (14):588-591; (15):634-635.

Swammerdam, Jan, 1732. Biblia Naturae, Leyden (Cited in Huber 1814).

Taber, Stephen III, 1954. The frequency of multiple mating of queen honey bees. Jour. Econ. Ent. 47(6):995-998.

Taber, S. III, 1955. Sperm distribution in the spermatheca of multiple mated queen honey bees. Jour. Econ. Ent. 48(5):522-525.

Taber, S. III, 1973. Influence of pollen location in the hive on its utilization by the honeybee colony. Jour. Apic. Res. 12(1):17-20.

Townsend, Gordon F., and Eva Crane, 1973. History of apiculture. In: History of Entomology, Annual Reviews, Inc., Palo Alto, California.

Townsend, O. H., 1880. Notes from the north shade apiary. How to get plenty of choice queen cells. Glean. Bee Cult. 8(7):322-323.

Tryasko, V. V., 1951. (Signs indicating the mating of queens.) Pchelovodstvo 28(11):25-31 (In Russian). Abstract by M. Simpson in Bee World 34:14 (1953).

Tryasko, V. V., 1957. (The mating sign of the queen and its characteristics.) Pchelovodstvo 34(4):22-28 (In Russian) Apic. Abstr., 186/58.

Tucker, K. W., 1958. Automictic parthenogenesis in the honey bee. Genetics 43:299-316.

Vesely, V., 1961. Towards the problem of artificial insemination of queen bees. Zoologické Listy (10):203-210 (Ref. from Ruttner 1976).

Vesely, V., 1970. Retention of semen in the lateral oviducts of artificially inseminated honey-bee queens, (Apis mellifera L.) Acta Entom. Bohemorl. 67(2):83-92 (Ref. from Ruttner 1976).

Wang, Der-I, 1965. Growth rates of young queen and worker honeybee larvae. Jour. Apic. Res. 4(1):3-5.

Wankler, Wilhelm, 1906. Die Königin. Wilhelm Wankler, Sulzberg (Boden).

Watson, Lloyd R., 1927. Controlled Mating of Queenbees. American Bee Journal, Hamilton, Illinois.

Weaver, N., 1955. Rearing of honey bee larvae on royal jelly in the laboratory. Science 121:509-510.

Weaver, Nevin, 1966. Physiology of caste determination. In: Ann. Rev. Ent. 11:79-102.

Wedmore, E. B., 1945. A Manual of Beekeeping for English-speaking Beekeepers. Edward Arnold and Company, London.

Weiss, K., 1975. Zur Kastenspezifische Ernährung der weiblichen Bienenlarvae (Apis mellifica, L). Apidologie 6(2):95-120 Apic. Abst. 1029/76.

West, N. D., 1906. The West spiral queen-cell protector. Glean. Bee Cult. 34 15):1056-1058.

Whitcomb, Warren, Jr., 1935. The shipping of package bees. USDA pub. E-363.

Whitcomb, Warren, Jr., (no date) Recommendations for shipping cages for bees. USDA publication E-287. (Publ. between 1930-1935.)

Wicht, Wm. W., 1947. Rearing better queens. Southern Beekeeper. I. 1(8):9-12; II. (9):11-14; III. (10):5-8; IV. (11):9-11.

Woodrow, A. W., 1941. Some effects of temperature, relative humidity, confinement, and type of food on queen bees in mailing cages. USDA publ. E-529.

Woyke, J., 1955. Multiple mating of the honeybee queen (Apis mellifica L.) in one nuptial flight. Bull. Acad. Polon. Sci. Ch. II 3(5):175-180.

Woyke, J., 1963a. Drone larvae from fertilized eggs of the honeybee. Jour. Apic. Res. 2(1):19-24.

Woyke, J., 1963b. What happens to diploid drone larvae in a honeybee colony. Jour. Apic. Res. 2(2):73-75.

Woyke, J., 1963c. The behaviour of queens inseminated artificially in different manner. XIXth International Beekeeping Congress Reports. Prague, pp. 702-703.

Woyke, J., 1967. Rearing conditions and the number of sperms reaching queen's spermatheca. XXI Intern. Beekeeping Congress, Maryland. pp. 232-234.

Woyke, J., 1971. Correlation between the age at which honeybee brood was grafted, characteristics of the resultant queens, and results of insemination. Jour. Apic. Res. 10(1):45-55.

Woyke, J., 1976. Population genetic studies on sex alleles in the honeybee using the example of the Kangaroo Island Bee Sanctuary. Jour. Apic. Res. 15 (3/4):105-123.

Woyke, J., 1977. Cannibalism and brood-rearing efficiency in the honeybee. Jour. Apic. Res. 16(1):84-94.

Woyke, J., and Z. Jasinski, 1973. Influence of external conditions on the number of spermatozoa entering the spermatheca of instrumentally inseminated honeybee queens. Jour. Apic. Res. 12(3):145-151.

Woyke, J., and F. Ruttner, 1958. An anatomical study of the mating process in the honeybee. Bee World 39(1):3-18.

Zander, Enoch, 1911. Der Bau der Biene, Verlagbuchhandlung, Eugen Ulmer. Stuttgart.

INDEX

A

Acarapis woodi, 175
Adam, A., 5, 162
Allelle, 141, 150-151
Alley, Henry, 32, 167, 168, 169, 170,
    172, 173, 175, 176
Alphonsus, E. C., 159, 165, 167, 171
Ambroise, Victor, 163
American Bee Journal, 166
Apis mellifera capensis, 162
Apis mellifera ligustica, 13
Apis mellifera mellifera, 13
Aristotle, 1, 18, 160
Artificial cell cups, 35-43
Audouin, M., 162

B

Baby nuclei, 89
Bee,
    black, 13, 166
    bread, 18
    Italian, 13, 166
    Length of developmental stages,
        Table 1, p. 19
    nurse, 18, 55, 58
Beekeeper management of test colonies,
    155-158
Beetsma, J., 17, 160
Benton, Frank, 176-177
Berlepsch, Baron von, 161
Bertholf, L. M., 19
Biology basic to queen rearing, 15-23,
    159-164
Biological phenomena underlying bee
    breeding, 148-158
Bishop, George, 12, 163
Black bee, *Apis mellifera mellifera,* 13
Board divides, 82
Boardman entrance feeder, 75
Bonnet, Charles, 163
Boyd, W. L., 168
Breeder colony,
    comb in breeder colony and to feeder
        colony, 44
    daily care of, 47-49
    manipulation of combs of, 47-49
    queen confined to compartment in
        shallow or 6⅝" body, 48; Fig.
        43, p. 49

queen confined to half-comb insert,
    Figs. 41, 42, pp. 47-48
queen confined to one or a few
    combs, 45; Fig. 39, p. 45
Smith, 32, 34
Breeding,
    biological phenomena underlying,
        148-155
    improvement of stock, 141-148
    maintenance of stock characteristics,
        140-141
    management of test colonies, 155-158
    queens, 13
    selection of queen and drone
        mothers, 14, 140-148, 156
Breeder queen,
    selection of, 14, 141, 155-158
Brooks, J. M., 167, 168, 170
Brewers yeast, 122
Briant, 4
Brood, spotty, 6
Brushing box, 136
Buchanan, J. A., 174
Bulk bee box, 86; *also see* Figs. 77-78,
    pp. 89-90
Bursa copulatrix, 2; *also see* Fig. 2, p. 3
Butler, Charles, 2, 159, 160, 161

C

Cages,
    candy for, 113
    comb, 101
    drone, maturing, 102
    first queen shipping cage, 175
    for package bees, 123; *also see* Fig.
        102, p. 124
    for post-insemination care of queens,
        Fig. 90, p. 105
    for shipping queens, Fig. 97, p. 112;
        Fig. 98, p. 113; Fig. 101, p. 117
    for shipping queens and drones to
        insemination centers, Fig. 92, p.
        108
    introducing, Fig. 91, p. 106
    Miller introducing, Fig. 91, p. 106;
        119
    nursery, Figs. 64-65, pp. 73-74
    Pinard, Fig. 97, p. 112; 115
    push-in, Fig. 91, 106; 118

queen, for packages, Fig. 97, p. 112;
Fig. 98, p. 113; Fig. 102, p. 124;
125
robber, 95; Fig. 86, p. 96
Caging queens, 109; *also see* Fig. 94, p.
110; Fig. 95 and Fig. 96, p. 111
Cale, 101; Fig. 91, p. 106
Camargo, C. A., 164
Camargo, J. M. F., 164
Candy,
first, 176
for queen cages, 113
formula for queen cage candy, 114-
115
Cannibalism, 6
Carbon dioxide,
use in instrumental insemination, 103
Caste,
determination, importance of food,
16-18
determination of queen, 15-18
development, importance of food,
15-18
divergence of developmental paths of
female castes, Fig. 12, p. 16
queen and worker, 15-18, 159-161
Catcher box,
for packages, Fig. 110, p. 131; Fig.
111, p. 132
Cell builders,
clustering room, 58; Fig. 52, p. 58
donor colonies, 57-59
early experiments with, 165-171
feeding of, 20, 58-59; Fig. 66, p. 75;
Fig. 67, p. 76; Fig. 68, p. 77
grouped in three rows, Fig. 69, p. 78
finishers, 66-68
starters, 55-66
starter-finisher, 68-72
Queenright, 68-70
modification of queenright starter-
finisher, 68-70; Fig. 60, p. 69
Queenless, 70-72
three colony cell finishing unit, 67-
68; Fig. 59, p. 67; Fig. 60, p. 69
Cell building,
building the cells, 30-35, 54-72
by queenless colonies, Fig. 6, p. 8;
30-32

by colony preparing to supersede, 20
by colony preparing to swarm, 20
by removing queen from colony,
30-32
conditions favorable for cell building,
20
early experiments with, 165-171
natural or spontaneous cells, 29
natural cells with beekeeper control,
30-32
Cell cups,
artificial, 20, 35-43
attachment of, 42
attachment to a bar, 37; *also see* Fig.
28, p. 37
bases of various, Fig. 29, p. 38
beeswax for, 35
dipping, 36-43; *also see* Fig. 27, p. 37
early experiments with, 170
forming stick for dipping, 36; Fig.
27, p. 37; 38, Fig. 30, p. 38; 39;
Fig. 31, p. 39
kinds of, Fig. 29, p. 38
multiple forming sticks, Fig. 30,
p. 38
natural, Fig. 5, p. 7
primed with royal jelly, Fig. 48,
p. 53
priming with royal jelly, 52-53
Cell finisher, 66-68; Fig. 60, p. 69;
Fig. 66, p. 75; Fig. 69, p. 78
Cell finisher, queenright, 66-68
Cell finishing unit, 67; Fig. 59, p. 67
Cell starter colony, confined 34, 55-61
Cell starter colony, free flying, 61-66
Cell starter colony with rim feeder,
64-66; Figs. 57-58, p. 65
Cell starter-finisher colonies, 68-72;
Fig. 61, p. 70
queenright starter-finisher, 68
modification of queenright starter-
finisher colony, 68-70
queenless starter-finisher colonies,
70-72
Cell starting body, Fig. 53, p. 60
Cell starting donor colonies, 57;
Fig. 56, p. 63
Cells, queen
building, 54-72

confined starter colonies for, 55-61
destroyed by virgin, Fig. 8, p. 9;
    Fig. 9, p. 10
double grafting, 54
drawn, 54; Fig. 6, p. 22; Fig. 49,
    p. 55
emerged, Fig. 10, p. 10
enlargement of worker, 7, 8; Fig. 6,
    p. 8
finishing, 54, 66-68; Fig. 59, p. 67;
    Fig. 60, p. 69; 68-72
incubation of, 54, 72
incubator for holding, 51; Fig. 62,
    p. 71; 73
incubator colony, 72
incubator rack, Fig. 63, p. 72
natural unsealed queen, Fig. 4, p. 6;
    Fig. 7, p. 9
removing bars from frames, 73
starting, 54-66
    cells 36 hours following grafting,
    Fig. 49, p. 55
    starter-finisher cell builders, 68
    queenright, 68-70; see also p. 66
    queenless, 70-72
swarm box, 56; Fig. 50, p. 56;
    Fig. 51, p. 57
swarm box modified, 59
Cells, reproductive and developmental
    division of egg, 15
    egg, Fig. 2, p. 3; Fig. 3, p. 5; Fig.
    13, p. 17
    follicle, 5; Fig. 3, p. 5
    nurse, 4; Fig. 3, p. 5
Chorion, 4; *also see* Fig. 13, p. 17; 148
Chromosomes, 149-151
Classification of queens, 13
Clipping queens, 115; *also see* Fig. 99,
    p. 114
Cocoon, Fig. 17, p. 23
Code, queen marking, 115
Colonies
    cell starting donor, 57, 63; *also see*
    Fig. 56, p. 63
    confined starter, 34, 55-61
    dividing, 81
    drone mother, 79-80, 100-101, 156
    feeding after shaking packages, 135;

    Figs. 115-116, pp. 134-135
    free-flying starter, 61-66
    modification of, 64; Figs. 57-58,
        p. 65
    increasing, 81
    management for package bees,
        121-123
    mating, 82-93, 96-108
    single story queenless cell starter-
        finisher, 70-72
    stock maintenance, 139-141
    test, management of, 155-158
    yard sheet, 146-148; Fig. 119, p. 144
Colony,
    breeder, 32, 34, 47-49, 140-148
    description or profiles, 141-148; Figs.
        118-119, pp. 143-144
    donor, 57-59; Figs. 56, p. 63
    drone mother, 79-80, 100-101, 156
    establishing package colony, 136-138
    establishing two-queen, 137-138
    incubator, 67, 72
    management for package bee
        production, 121-123
    modification of free-flying starter,
        64-66
    preparation of cell building,
        31-34, 54-72
    queen, mother of, 1, 151
    queen storage in, 112-113
    queenless, 1
    queenright, 1
    queenright-finishing, 66-68
    rating method, 145-148
    relationship of drones in, 152
    relationship of individuals in, 151
    relationship of workers in, 152-156;
        Figs. 120-123, pp. 153-156
    requeening, 29, 121
    "robber screen," 81
    "stack," 55
    starter, 34, 54-66
    three colony cell finishing unit,
        67-68; Figs. 59, p. 67; Fig. 60,
        p. 69
Colvin, Richard, 175
Comb,
    in breeder colony, 44
    to feeder colony, 44

Confined starter colonies, 55-61
  modified swarm box, 59-61
  swarm box, 56-61
Controlled mating, 96, 163
Cook, 175
Corn syrup, isomerized, for candy, 114
Crane, Eva, 159-160

D

Dadant, C. P., 165, 175
Davis, J. L., 168
Development of queen rearing as a
    commercial beekeeping activity,
    166-177
Developmental stages, Table 1, p. 19
Dietz, A., 17
Divide board, 82; Fig. 71, p. 83
Divided standard hive body nuclei,
    84-89
Divides, 81-82, 171-172
Division screen, 62; *also see* Fig. 55,
    p. 62
Divisions, 171-172
Donor colonies, 57-59; Fig. 56, p. 63
Doolittle, G. M., 35, 168-171, 173-174
  division board feeder, 75; also see
      Fig. 53, p. 60; Fig. 75, p. 87;
      Fig. 80, p. 91; Fig. 82, p. 92;
      Fig. 115, p. 134
Double grafting, 54
Doull, Keith, 18
Drivert,® 84, 85, 113-114, 116, 122
  for queen cage candy, 113-114
Drones,
  and fertilization of eggs, 161-162
  and parthenogenesis, 6, 161
  cages for maturing in a nursery
      colony, 102; Fig. 89, p. 102
  comb cage for emerging in an
      incubator, 101; Fig. 88, p. 101
  development of, 6; Table 1, p. 19
  die at mating, 12
  diploid, 6
  eliminating from packages, 127-132
  emergence in feeding colonies, 101
  emergence in incubator, 101-102
  for mating, 79-80
  haploid, 150

judging maturity of, 100
length of developmental stages,
    Table 1, p. 19
mating, 12
matured in cages, 101-103
maturing, 12, 100-103, 150
mother colonies, 79-80, 100-101, 156
origin and maturation of
    spermatozoa, 149-150
origin of, 6, 150, 161
relationship within colony, 152
securing mature, 100-103
selected drone mothers, 100, 156
sperm development, 11, 149-150
Dry grafting, 52, 170
DuPraw, E. J., 15
Dzierzon, Johannes, 6, 161, 172, 175

E

Earliest methods of rearing queens, 165
Eckert, J. E., 4
Egg-laying,
  after mating, 11
  commencement of, 11
  environmental influences, 6
  influence of seasonal change upon, 6
  in natural cell cups, 7
  rate of, 4, 7
  role of food in, 6
Eggs, 4-5, 15
  eggs, shape and size, Fig. 13, p. 17
  cell divisions, 149
  cellular envelope of, 4; Fig. 3, p. 5
  development of 4; Fig. 3, p. 5
  drones and fertilization of, 161
  embryogeny, 15
  embryonic development of, 15
  fertilization of 5, 6, 161-162
  maturation, 148, 149
  origin, 4, 15, 148, *see also* Fig. 2,
      p. 3; Fig. 3, p. 5
  yolk, 15
Embryo cell cups, 168
Emergence of queen rearing as a
    beekeeping practice, 165-166
Emergency cells, Fig. 6, p. 8; Fig. 7,
    p. 9; 30
Endophallus, 12

Epithelium, 5
Excluder,
    confinement of breeder queen, 32,
        34, 45-49; Fig. 39, p. 45; Figs.
        41-43, pp. 47-49; Fig. 43, p. 49
    donor colonies, 57-59
    drones from packages, 127-132
    for establishing nuclei, 83
    partitions to confine queen, 32-34,
        45-49; Fig. 39, p. 45; Figs. 41-
        43, pp. 47-49
    queenright cell builder, 66-70
Expedient and hobby queen rearing,
    29-35

F

Feeders,
    Boardman entrance, 75
    Doolittle division board, 59; Fig. 53,
        p. 60; 61, 75
    feeder screen, 76; Fig. 68, p. 77
    jar, 56; Fig. 50, p. 56
    Park, 75; *also see* Figs. 66-67,
        pp. 75-76
    rim, 64; *also see* Fig. 58, p. 65
Feeding,
    breeder colony larvae, 44-45
    cans for package cages, 125; *also see*
        Fig. 103, p. 125
    donor colonies, 58
    finisher colonies, 66-68
    incubator colony, 72
    large scale, Fig. 115, p. 134;
        Fig. 116, p. 135
    nuclei, 84-85
    nursery colonies, 74
    of larvae, 18, 19
    package bees before shipment, 136
    package colonies after shaking, 135
    packages, 124
    packages at installation, 137
    starter colonies, 55-56, 59, 61, 63-64
    starter-finisher colonies, 71
Fertilization of eggs, 5, 161-162
Finishing the cells, 54, 66-68
    queenright finishing colony, 66-68
Flanders, S. E., 4
Follicle cell, 5; Fig. 3, p. 5

Foti, N., 106
Fradenburg, A. A., 174
Fraser, Henry Malcolm, 177
Free-flying starter colonies, 61-66
    modification of, 64
Fryer, J., 177
Fumidil B, 137
Functioning or expression of genes,
    150-151

G

Gametes, 152, 154, 155
Garófalo, C. A., 6
Genes,
    expression of, 150-151
    functioning of, 150-151
Genetics, 139-140
Gerry E., 172
Glands,
    brood food, 18
    hypopharyngeal, 18
    spermathecal, Fig. 2, p. 3
Gleanings in Bee Culture, 166
Goncalves, L. S., 164
Good, I. R., 176
Grafting, 34, 35, 46, 48-54; Fig. 47,
    p. 53; 168
    "automatic" needle, 51; Fig. 46,
        p. 52
    double, 54
    "dry," 52
    house, 49; Figs. 44-45, p. 50
    humidity for, 49, 51
    into artificial cups, 51
    into natural cups, 51
    into "primed" cell cups, 53
    light for, 51
    needles, 51-52
    record, 76-78
    size of larvae for, 20; Fig. 15, p. 22
    "straight" needle, 51; Fig. 46, p. 52
    temperature, 49
Grimm, Adam, 175

H

Half-comb insert, 47-48; Figs. 41-42,
    pp. 47-48
Heredity, queen custodian, 1

History of queen rearing in the United
    States, 159-177
Hive,
    breeder, 32, 34, 44-49
    records, 120
    seat, Fig. 93, p. 109
Hobby queen rearing, 29-31, 66, 68
Huber, Francis, 159, 160, 161, 162, 163,
    165, 168, 171
Hypopharyngeal glands, 18

I

Improvement of stock, 141-158
Increase, 81-82
Incubator, 51; Fig. 62, p. 71
    colony, 67, 72
    comb cage for emerging drones,
        Fig. 88, p. 101
    rack with bars of queen cells,
        Fig. 63, p. 72
Individual queen records, 142, 145-148;
    Fig. 118, p. 143
In Retrospect, 177
Insemination laboratories, 107
Installation of package bees, 136-138
Instrumental insemination of queens,
    96-108
    early attempts, 163-164
    introduction of queens, 106-107
    planning the inseminations, 98-100;
        Fig. 87, p. 99
    post-insemination care, 104-106
    pre-insemination care, 103-104
    sanitation, 97
    scheduling form for, 98; *also see*
        Fig. 87, p. 99
Intercastes, 16-18
International queen marking color
    code, 115
Introducing cages, Fig. 91, p. 106
Introduction,
    of instrumentally inseminated queens,
        106-107
    of queens, 118-120
    push-in cage, 118; Fig. 91, p. 106
Isomerized high fructose corn syrup,
    114
Italian bee, 13, 175

J

Jacob, Michael, 159
Jansha, A., 159, 160, 162, 163, 165,
    167, 169, 171
Jay, Cameron S., 24; Table 2, p. 26
Jaycox, E. R., 12
Jelly spoon, 53
Jones, D. A., 171
Jurine, Miss, 159

K

Koeniger, N., 6, 164

L

Laidlaw, H. H., 1, 4, 12, 13, 17, 18,
    98, 100, 101, 105, 153, 154, 155,
    156, 164
Langstroth, L. L., 160, 162, 166, 167,
    171, 172, 175
Larch, E. C., 168
Larva, 6
    caste development, 16-17
    divergence between queen and
        workers, 16-17
    divergence of developmental paths,
        16; Fig. 12, p. 16
    feeding of, 18, 20
    feeding on royal jelly, Frontispiece;
        Fig. 18, p. 24
    hatching, 15; Fig. 15, p. 21
    moulting, 20-21; Table 1, p. 19
    newly sealed, Fig. 17, p. 23
    queen and worker divergence,
        Fig. 12, p. 16
    selection of in queenless colonies, 8;
        Fig. 6, p. 8
    uncommitted upon hatching, 15
Larvae, 6
    age for grafting, 20
    early experiments with obtaining for
        grafting, 167
    embryonic development, 15
    feeding of, 18, 20
    grafting size of, 20; Fig. 15, p. 22
    growth of, 20-21, also see Table 1,
        p. 19; Fig. 16, p. 22
    newly hatched, Fig. 14, p. 21

obtaining for grafting 20, 34, 43-49
post-embryonic development, 15-18
right size and age for grafting,
    Fig. 15, p. 22
Larval food, 17
Lateral oviducts, 2; Fig. 2, p. 3; 4-5,
    148, 164
Leuckart, C. T. E. von, 162

M

Mackensen, Otto, 98, 104, 162, 164
Mahan, P. G., 175
Maintenance of stock, 139-141
Manum, A. E., 177
Marking queens, 115; Fig. 100, p. 116
International color code for, 115
Mating, 11-13
    colonies or nuclei, 82-93
    control of, 96-108, 139
    death of drones, 12
    early experiments with, 171-174
    flights, 11-13
    flights, multiple, first discovery of,
        164
    from "board divides," 82; Fig. 71,
        p. 83
    from full size hives, 80
    instrumental insemination, 96-108,
        163-164
    multiple, 11-13, 164
    nuclei, 82-93
        records, 93, 95
    of the queen, 162
    providing mates, 79-80
    sign, 12
Mating the queen, 79
    instrumental insemination, 96
Mating yard layout and records, 93
Maturation of eggs, 148-149
Maturation of spermatozoa, 149-150
McLain, Nelson, 163
Median oviduct, 4
Mello, M. L. S., 164
Mendez de Torres, Luiz, 160
Miller, C. C., 31, 167
    introducing cage, Fig. 91, p. 106;
        119
    method of queen rearing, Fig. 24,
        p. 30; 31

Modified swarm box, 59
    variation of, 61
Modification of free-flying starter
    colony, 64-65
Murry, H. D., 13
Micropyle of egg, 5

N

Nelson, J. A., 15
Newton, Sir Isaac, 177
Nolan, W. J., 164, 176
Nuclei, mating, 82-93, 171-174
    baby, 89-93; Figs. 79, 80, p. 91; 81,
        82, p. 92; Fig. 85, p. 94
    care of combs overwinter, 90, 93;
        Fig. 76, p. 88; Fig. 83, p. 93
    dead outs, 84, 89
    divided standard hive body, 84-85;
        Fig. 73, p. 85; Fig. 75, p. 87;
        172
    double baby, Fig. 81, p. 92
    early experiments with, 171, 172,
        173, 174
    establishing, 81-83, 85-86, 89
    feeding, 84; Fig. 75, p. 87; Fig. 80,
        p. 91; Fig. 82, p. 92; 116-117
    loss of queens from, 174
    mating yard layout, 93, 95
    re-celling, 116-117
    reconditioning, 84, 89
    shallow body divided crosswise, 85;
        Fig. 74, p. 86
    single full-depth or shallow standard
        frame, 83; Fig. 73, p. 85
    standard five-frame, 83; Fig. 72,
        p. 84
    ventilation of, 89
Nucleus
    Box, conversion to swarm box, 56
    for feeding larvae, 45
    stool, 109
    yards, Figs. 84-85, p. 94
Nucleus, cell, 5, 15
Nulomoline®
    for queen cage candy, 113, 114
Nurse bees, 18
Nurse cells, 4, 5
Nursery cages, Fig. 64, p. 73

Nursery cages in colony, Fig. 65, p. 74
  drone cages for maturing drones,
    Fig. 89, p. 102
Nurseries, for virgins, 73-75

O

Obed, 167, 172
Oertel, E., 164
Oocyte, 5, 148
Oogenesis, Fig. 3, p. 5; 148
Oogonium, 5; Fig. 3, p. 5
Onions, G. W., 162
Ovaries, 2; Fig. 2, p. 3; 4, 148
  of queen, Fig. 2, p. 3
Ovarioles, 4; Fig. 2, p. 3; Fig. 3,
    p. 5; 148
  number of, 4
Oviduct,
  of queen, 2; Fig. 2, p. 3; 5
Oviposition, 4-7
  controlled by workers, 6
  rate of, 4, 7

P

Package bees,
  cages for, 123-124; Fig. 102, p. 124
  caging queens for, 125
  colony management, 121-123
  catcher box for, 130-132; Fig. 110,
    p. 131; Fig. 111, p. 132
  crating, 132-135; Figs. 113-114,
    pp. 133-134
  eliminating drones from, 127-132
  elimination of hitch hiking bees, 135-
    136; *also see* Fig. 117, p. 136
  feeding before shipment, 136
  feeder cans for, 123-124; Fig. 103,
    p. 125
  filling cages, 124-135
  installation of, 136-138
  production, 121-138
  queens caged for, 112-113
  shaker box, 128; Figs. 105-108,
    pp. 127, 129, 130
  supplies, 123-124
  weighing, 127; Fig. 106, p. 129; Fig.
    109, p. 131; 132; Fig. 112,
    p. 133

Park feeder for cell building colonies,
    75; Figs. 66-67, pp. 75-76
Parthenogenesis, 6, 161
Parsons, S. B., 175
Peet shipping and introducing cage,
    177
Pellett, F. C., 175, 176
Penis, 12
Pheromones, 1, 104, 118
Phillips, E. F., 175, 176
Pinard cage, 115, 123; Figs. 94-98
    pp. 110-113
Piping, of virgins, 8
Pollen, 18
  feeding screen, 76; Fig. 68, p. 77
  filled combs, Fig. 38, p. 44
  mixing with supplements, 121-122
  for starter colonies, 55-66
  supplements, for package bee
    production, 121-122
Posel, 162
Pre-insemination care of virgins,
    103-104
Prepupa, 24; *also see* Fig. 19, p. 25
Priming cell cups with royal jelly,
    52-53; Fig. 48, p. 53
Pritchard, 168
Pupa, 24; Fig. 20, p. 25; Fig. 21, p. 26
  color changes, Table 2, p. 26
Push-in cage, 118-119; Fig. 91, p. 106

Q

Queen, breeding, selection of, 14, 141,
    155-158
Queen, Fig. 1, p. 2
  cages, Fig. 97, p. 112
  cage candy, 113-115
    formula for, 114
  caging, 109-115; Fig. 94, p. 110;
    Figs. 95-96, p. 111
  caste, 159-161
  caste determination, 15-18
    divergence of developmental paths
      of queen and worker, Fig. 12,
      p. 16
  cell,
    after emergence of virgin, Fig. 10,
      p. 10

appearance of, Fig. 4, p. 6; Fig. 7, p. 9; Figs. 16-22, pp. 22-27; Fig. 49, p. 55

cups, *see cell cups*

destruction of, by unconfined queen, Figs. 8-9, pp. 9-10

emerged, Fig. 10, p. 10

flaring of walls of worker comb, Fig. 6, p. 8

growth of, 21; Figs. 16, p. 22; 17, p. 23; 18, p. 24; 19-20, p. 25; 20, p. 26; 22, p. 27

in nature, Fig. 4, p. 6; Fig. 6, p. 8; Fig. 7, p. 9

incubator for, 73; Fig. 62, p. 71; Fig. 63, p. 72

larval growth, Table 1, p. 19; Fig. 16, p. 22

natural, 6; Fig. 4, p. 6; Fig. 6, p. 8; Fig. 7, p. 9; 29

newly sealed, Fig. 17, p. 23

records for, 76-78

requeening with, 80-81

spontaneous, 29-30

webbed, Fig. 40, p. 46

clipping, 115; Fig. 99, p. 114

clipping and marking, 115-116

confinement of breeder, 45-49

custodian of heredity, 1

description of mating, 12

determination of caste, 15-18

divergence of developmental path, Fig. 12, p. 16

effect on colony, 1

egg-laying, sex of eggs, 6
rate, 4, 7

eggs, Fig. 13, p. 17

emergence of virgin, 8, 28; Fig. 10, p. 10

fertilization of eggs, 5, 6, 161-162

first discovery as female, 1, 160

influence on workers, 1, 2

introduction,
Miller cage, Fig. 91, p. 106; 119
push-in cage, 106, 118-119

life span, 1

marking, 115

mated to one drone, 152-153; *also see* Fig. 120, p. 153

mated to several drones from different mothers, 153; Fig. 121, p. 154

mated to several drones from same mother, 153-154; *also see* Fig. 122, p. 155

mated to drones from different mothers and also drones from same mother, 154; *also see* Fig. 123, p. 156

mates, 11, 79-80

mating of, 11-13, 79, 162, 171-174

mating sign, 12

mother of colony, 1

newly emerged, Fig. 23, p. 27

origin of, 7

ovaries of, 2; Fig. 2, p. 3; 4

pheromones, 1, 104, 118

post-insemination care, 104

pre-insemination care, 103

providing mates for, 79-80

record, Fig. 118, p. 143-148

rearing,
biological basis of, 15-28, 159-164
development of as commercial beekeeping activity, 166-177
Doolittle method, 35
emergence of as a beekeeping practice, 165-166
expedient, 29-35
larval feeding colonies for, 44-49
grafting, 34-35, 46, 48-54, 168
history of, 159-177
hobby, 29-35
importance of young larva, 18
Miller method, 31-32; Fig. 24, p. 30
obtaining larvae, 43-49
Smith system, 32-34; Figs. 25, 26, p. 33

recognition of worker and drone cells, 6, 164

relationship within colony, 151-158

removal, effect on colony, 1

reproductive system and sting, Fig. 2, p. 3

reproductive tract, 2-4

role in the colony, 1

shipping cages, Fig. 97, p. 112

spermatheca, Fig. 2, p. 3; 4, 5, 155, 162, 164

storage in a bank colony, 112-113; Fig. 98, p. 113

yard stool, 109; Fig. 93, p. 109

Queenless colonies,
   selection of larvae to become queens, 8; *also see* Fig. 6, p. 8

Queenless starter-finisher colonies, 70-72

Queenright cell finisher, 66-68; variation, see Fig. 60, p. 69

Queenright starter-finishers, 68-70

Queens,
   breeding queens, 14
   caged for package bees, 112; Fig. 98, p. 113
   cages for shipping, Fig. 97, p. 112
   caging, 109; Figs. 94-96, pp. 110-111
   caging for packages, 125
   classification, 13-14
   clipping and marking, 115-116
   color changes in pupae, Table 2, p. 26
   early experiments with mating, 171-174
   fighting virgins, Fig. 11, p. 11
   first package shipping of season, 126
   handling, 110
   improvement, 139-158
   improvement of stock, 139-158
   individual records, 142-148
   insemination laboratories for, 107-108
   introduction of, 106-107, 118-120
   introduction of instrumentally inseminated, 98, 106-107, 118-120
   length of developmental stages, Table 1, p. 19
   maintenance of characteristics, 140-141
   marking, 115-116; Fig. 100, p. 116
   mating by instrumental insemination, 96-108
   mating flights, 11-13
   mating from full size hives, 80-82
   mismating of, 13
   multiple mating, 11, 13
   origin and maturation of eggs, 148-149
   origin of, 4, 148-149; *see also* Fig. 2, p. 3; Fig. 3, p. 5
   oviposition of instrumentally inseminated queens, 103
   post-insemination care of instrumentally inseminated, 104
   pre-insemination care of instrumentally inseminated, 103
   production of virgin, 29-78
   shipping, 117-118; Fig. 101, p. 117
   select tested, 13
   selection of breeding stock, 156-157
   stock maintenance, 139-141
   storage in a bank colony, 112; Fig. 98, p. 113
   tested, 13
   untested, 13
   use of, 109-120

Quinby, M., 175

R

Rating, colony, 145-148

Rearing virgin queens, first attempts, 165-166

Reaumur, R.A.F., 162

Re-celling, 116-117

Records,
   graft, 76-78
   hive, 120
   individual queen, 142-146; Fig. 118, p. 143
   mating yard, 93-95
   nucleus, 95
   planning, instrumental insemination, 98, 100; Fig. 87, p. 99
   yard sheet, 146-148; Fig. 119, p. 144

Remnant, Richard, 159

Reproductive system and sting of queen, Fig. 2, p. 3

Reproductive tract of queen, 2-4

Requeening, 29, 80-81, 121

Riem, 159

Rim feeder, 64; Fig. 58, p. 65

Robber cage, Fig. 86, p. 96

Robber screen, 81-83; Fig. 70, p. 81; 95
   Steve Taber screen, Fig. 79, p. 91

Robbing, 95-96

Roberts, W. C., 164
Robinson, C. J., 166, 175
Root, A. I., 167, 168, 170, 172,
   175, 177
Rose, W. G., 175
Rothenbuhler, W. C., 141
Royal jelly, 17, 18, 21; Frontispiece;
   Figs. 15-16, p. 22; Figs. 18-22,
   pp. 24-27
Rutner, F., 12, 13, 98, 164

S

Schirach, A. G., 159, 160, 165
Scholz, 176
Scholz-Good candy, 177
Screen, division, Fig. 55, p. 62
Screen, pollen feeding, Fig. 68, p. 77
Screen, robber, 81-82; Fig. 70, p. 81;
   Fig. 79, p. 91; 95
Select tested queens, 13
Selection of breeding queens, 14, 141,
   155-158
Seminal vesticles, 11
Sex control, 5
Shaker box, 127-132; Fig. 105, p. 127;
   Figs. 106-111, pp. 129-133
Shaw, F. R., 174
Shipping cage for package bees,
   Fig. 102, p. 124
Shipping queens, 117; Fig. 101, p. 117
Shuel *et al.*, 160
Significance of honey bee relationships,
   154-155
Smith, Jay, 32, 119
   breeder hive, Figs. 25-26, p. 33
Smith, 176
Snodgrass, R. E., 2, 3, 4, 5, 11, 12
Soybean flour, 122
Sperm, 4
   development of, 11-12, 149-150
Spermatheca, 4, Fig. 2, p. 3
Spermathecal duct, 4
Spermatozoa,
   formation, 11-12, 149-150
   maturation of, 149
   migration, 12
   origin of, 149-150
Spiral cell protector, 173

Spotty brood, 6
Starter-finisher cell builders, 68-72
Starter-finisher colonies, queenless,
   70-72
Starting the cells, 54-72
   confined starter colonies, 55-61
   free-flying starter colonies, 61-66
Sting,
   of queens, Fig. 2, p. 3
   of queen, role in oviposition, 4
Sting chamber, 2
Stock,
   improvement of, 139-140, 141-158
   maintenance, 139-141
   maintenance of characteristics,
      140-141
Stool, nucleus, 109; Fig. 93, p. 109
Storing queens in a bank colony, 112,
   113; Fig. 98, p. 113
Sugar syrup, 122
   for cell builders, 20
   for nuclei, 84
   invert for queen cage candy, 113
Super horse, 59; Fig. 54, p. 61
Super sisters, 153; Fig. 12, p. 153
Swammerdam, 160, 161
Swarm box, 56; Fig. 50, p. 56
   donor or support colonies, 57
   food for, Fig. 51, p. 57
   stocking of, 57
Swarming box, 168
Swarming,
   cell building, 20
   queenright cell builders, 58
   support colonies, 58
   virgins held in cells, 8
Swarms, as colony replacements, 165
Syrup, 124; Fig. 115, p. 134; Fig. 116,
   p. 135
   type-50, 114, 122, 124

T

Taber, S., 18, 155, 164
   robber screen, Fig. 79, p. 91
Test colonies, beekeeper management,
   155-158
Tested queens, 13
Testes, 11

Tool, grafting, 51-54; Fig. 46, p. 52
Torres, de, 160
Torula brewers yeast, 122
Torutein-10,® 122
Townley, J. H., 175
Townsend, G., 159, 160
Townsend and Crane, 159-160
Townsend, O. H., 167
Tucker, K. W., 98, 162
Tryasko, V. V., 12, 164

U

Untested queens, 13

V

Vagina, 2, 4
Valvefold, 4, 12
  discovery as an obstruction in
    artificial insemination, 164
Vesely, V., 164
Virgin queens,
  destruction of queen cells, 8;
    Fig. 9, p. 10
  emergence of, 8; Fig. 10, p. 10;
    Fig. 23, p. 27
Virgins,
  fighting, 8; Fig. 11, p. 11
  mating flight, 11, 163-164
  mating of, 11, 79-106
  multiple mating, 11, 164
  nurseries, 73-75
  piping, 8

  pre-insemination care of, 103
  production of, 29-78
von Planta, A., 160
von Siebold, C. T. E., 162

W

Wagner, Samuel, 175
Watson, Lloyd, 164
Weaver, N., 17
Weigel, 176
West, N. D., 173
Woodrow, A. W., 177
Worker,
  caging attendant, Fig. 96, p. 111
  caste, 15-18, 159-161
  divergence of developmental paths,
    Fig. 12, p. 16
  first discovery as female, 159
  length of developmental stages,
    Table 1, p. 19
  relationship within colony, 152-155;
    Figs. 120-123, pp. 153-156
Woyke, J., 6, 12, 13, 18, 141, 156, 164

Y

Yard sheet, 146; *also see* Fig. 119,
    p. 144
Yeast, 122

Z

Zander, Enoch, 163